How Jazz came to China

Whitey Smith

with
C.L. McDermott

and
a new introduction by Andrew Field

I Didn't Make A Million
By Whitey Smith

ISBN-13: 978-988-8769-33-9

© 2017 Whitey Smith

New Introduction © 2017 Andrew Field

This book has been reset in 10pt Book Antiqua. Spellings and punctuations are left as in the original edition.

HISTORY / Asia / China

EB084

All rights reserved. No part of this book may be reproduced in material form, by any means, whether graphic, electronic, mechanical or other, including photocopying or information storage, in whole or in part. May not be used to prepare other publications without written permission from the publisher except in the case of brief quotations embodied in critical articles or reviews. For information contact info@earnshawbooks.com

Published by Earnshaw Books Ltd. (Hong Kong)

Foreword
by Andrew Field

SHANGHAI WAS THEN and remains today a magnet for people looking to make a quick fortune. Many of those who come to try their luck fail, and with those who make it, many are too careless or feckless to cash in their chips while the going is good. That was Whitey Smith. Whitey was talented, charming and artistic, a drummer from San Francisco who landed in China's most flamboyant city just as it was ready to launch into its own version of the Roaring Twenties. Outside of a small circle of foreigners, jazz was unheard of in China, but Whitey was determined to change that. And he did.

Whitey arrived in Shanghai in 1922, with no thought of being here more than a short while to make some money before returning Stateside. He ended up spending the rest of his life in Asia. That's a familiar story for foreigners even today.

He was born into a Danish family that emigrated to the USA when he was a boy, and grew up in the San Francisco Bay Area, where he experienced the great earthquake of 1906. He came of age in the 1910s, when jazz was the breakout musical style. He took up drumming in a jazz band, as well as boxing and selling newspapers. It was the drumming that provided a future. His fate was sealed when a cafe owner from Shanghai named Louis Ladow walked into the club he was playing at in San Francisco and invited him to cross the Pacific.

Like most good storytellers recounting their life stories,

I DIDN'T MAKE A MILLION

Whitey Smith embellishes on more than one occasion. Did he really singlehandedly "teach China to dance?" as the Nobel Prize-winning novelist, Pearl Buck, later claimed? Well, yes and no.

In the 1920s, there were other American musicians and dancers in Shanghai teaching young Chinese how to do the fox-trot, the Charleston and the rumba. But it is also true that of all the spots where Chinese were first learning to dance, the Majestic Hotel, where Whitey and his band performed, was the most significant. And it's also true that he played at the wedding of Generalissimo Chiang Kai-shek and Mei-ling Soong on December, 1, 1927. Talk about a historic gig.

Whitey Smith's story of adjusting American jazz music to suit Chinese ears, told in Chapter 5, is pure gold for fans of the Jazz Age. In the 1920s, jazz was spreading like wildfire around the globe, and all it took was a bit of fanning to carry the flames to Chinese Shanghai. By simplifying the complex harmonies of orchestrated jazz, bringing out the main melody, and incorporating some Chinese folk tunes into his repertoire, Whitey played at least as big a role as any other non-Chinese musician in hastening the dawn of the China's own Jazz Age. He may have even directly influenced the Shanghai-based impresario and song-writer Li Jinhui, whose jazzy Chinese music was widely branded "yellow" (pornographic) in the early 1930s. Li became in the end the precursor of Chinese pop music in Hong Kong and Taiwan in the 1960s and 1970s, its influence finally circling back to the mainland in the 1980s through the sweet ballads of Taiwanese songstress Teresa Teng (Deng Lijun).

Listening to the Whitey Smith Orchestra's original tune "Nighttime in Old Shanghai," one hears the "sweet jazz" of 1920s white America, with a "Chinese" touch. But it wasn't until slightly later after other musicians arrived, namely Jack Carter,

FOREWORD

Teddy Weatherford, Valaida Snow, and Buck Clayton and his Harlem Gentlemen, that Shanghai experienced the authentic sounds of black American jazz artists. Even so, Whitey had ever right to his claim of being the pioneer.

In his memoir, Whitey recounts the tale of Buck Clayton being punched out at the Canidrome Ballroom by the notorious gangster, Jack Riley, in 1934. But puzzlingly, he doesn't mention the famous African-American jazz trumpet player by name. A touch of competitiveness, perhaps? He also gives little if any attention to the Russian, Filipino, and Japanese orchestras that filled the city's dance halls in those years and ignores Chinese musicians like Li Jinhui. Nor does he have much to say about the Chinese songstresses who made jazz a household word in Shanghai. It's a slightly myopic view, but it's his story, and we can forgive Whitey for his self-centered approach to Shanghai's Jazz Age. He was, after all, a product of his times. And the tales he does tell are full of both fun and tragedy, with a pervading tone of self-deprecating humor.

We can also forgive Whitey for not being more conscious of the revolutionary forces that were roiling around him. He had little regard for the Communist Party, and unlike the journalists who wrote memoirs of the era, he has little to say about the great political movements of the age. Throughout his memoir, one encounters scattered and brief references to major historical figures like Chiang Kai-shek and Green Gang boss Du Yuesheng, as well as events like the May Thirtieth Movement of 1925, the Nationalist Revolution of 1927, and the Zhabei War of 1932, all of which rocked Shanghai. But many of the foreigners were not really paying much attention. As to Whitey, it seems he was too busy trying to make folks happy through his music to read the writing on the wall of history.

Whitey Smith left Shanghai in 1937 just before the Japanese

I DIDN'T MAKE A MILLION

invaded central China and took over much of the International Settlement, moving to Manila. But he remained in Asia despite all the warning signs, and continued to play jazz, set up and run night clubs and make people merry through revolution, upheavals and war, until he was finally incarcerated in a Japanese prison camp in the Philippines in the early 1940s. He stayed on in Manila at the end of the war, and spent the rest of his life there running a small cafe. He died around 1970.

All in all, this memoir is the best personal account of the 1920s and 1930s Jazz Age in Shanghai, written by a non-Chinese musician from those times, and also the most readable. We are lucky he bothered to write it all down.

Andrew David Field
author of *Shanghai's Dancing World* and *Shanghai Nightscapes*
Shanghai
April 2017

Introduction

THE FIRST TIME I saw Whitey Smith, perspiration was running down his face. It was hot in the Majestic Hotel Ballroom and Whitey was so nervous you would have thought it was his own wedding. Generalissimo Chiang Kai-shek by contrast looked cool as a cucumber under all the photographers' lights, standing beside his beautiful bride, Soong Mei-ling.

It was in Shanghai in 1927. Whitey was at the top of his career as a band leader. With his twenty-two young American musicians he had been asked to play at Chiang's wedding. It was the most pretentious social function of its kind in that year of years for the Generalissimo. Chiang had just come up from the south and taken over the city in the name of Dr. Sun Yat Sen.

Whitey was a blue-eyed Danish-American with white-blond hair and a boyish face. He was an institution in the entertainment world up and down the China Coast in the lush days of the nineteen twenties and thirties. At one time he had three bands in Shanghai and one in Hong Kong run by his brother Holger. The famous author Pearl Buck once said Whitey did China more good than a bundle of ambassadors because he taught the Chinese how to dance.

Whitey was born Sven Eric Heinrich Schmidt in the little town of Vejle, Denmark. His parents brought him to America when he was just old enough to learn thirty words of English from the funny papers. He and his family were almost buried alive in the San Francisco earthquake. He has been a professional boxer

I DIDN'T MAKE A MILLION

(once bantam champion of Oakland, California), a newsboy, golf caddy, pool ball racker, drummer, bartender, soldier, radio announcer, salesman, promoter, winner, loser, and married at least twice. He was christened Whitey Smith by a newsboy.

He has two characteristics which have kept him in hot water a good deal of his life. He has a heart as big as a house and he always wanted like the devil to make a million dollars. When his friends are in need they come to Whitey, and they are legion. If he hadn't been so impulsively generous all his life he might have made –and kept - a million. I would not be surprised if he has made it, and given it away.

Whitey has lived through and set down in this book a span of violent history that so far as I know has never before been compressed and brought to life. He was right at the core of night life in fabulous Shanghai in the days before World War Two. He knew more world celebrities than the rulers of the country knew. He played with celebrities and for them. They danced to his music and they became his friends.

All the international conflicts in Asia since the days of the war lords have exploded around Whitey's blond head and left him alive to tell about them. The Communist uprisings of the twenties gave him several narrow escapes from death. The repercussions of the Manchurian Incident in 1931 put him out of business when he was broke and struggling to make a comeback. He squeaked out of Chefoo on a U.S. naval vessel in 1937 one jump ahead of the Japanese war on China, a refugee. He was caught by World War Two in Manila and spent three years in Santo Tomas internment camp. From hobnobbing with the great and near-great he went to boiling banana roots to keep from starving to death.

I will never know what kept Whitey Smith from being snowed under in the wild, uninhibited final days of Shanghai before the Bamboo Curtain dropped. Whitey has more bounce than

INTRODUCTION

a golf ball. Two priceless assets have remained to him through vicissitude and temptation. He has untarnished integrity and he has a sense of humor. When Whitey is happy everybody around him is happy. When he's low and broke you will never know it if he can help it, and he usually can. He told me that the three years it took him to set down the material in this book were among the happiest of his life.

Maybe Whitey Smith didn't make a million dollars but he made a million friends and a million laughs. Lots of them are right here in the following pages. Now go on and enjoy yourself.

Ford Wilkins
Manila, 1956

Whitey Smith acting as best man at one of many Shanghai weddings

1

IN THE YEAR 1922 I knew just as much about China as China knew about me. I had been down in Los Angeles for a year playing the Coconut Grove in the Ambassador Hotel. I was back in San Francisco with Max Bradfield at Tait's, on O'Farrell Street, across from the Orpheum Theater. Upstairs was Fanchon and Marco's place called the Little Club. I got a job playing there when I wasn't working for Max, and this meant I had to move my drums twice a day. Rube Wolf was in charge at the Little Club. He was a brother of Fanchon and Marco, also a trumpet player and comedian.

The two jobs were a lot of fun but neither one was a sure thing because of prohibition. There were always rumors that the place would be transformed into a coffee shop and restaurant with no room for bottles under the table, so when I got up each morning I was always wondering whether I would have one job, two jobs or no job at all at the end of the day.

For several nights in a row I had noticed a steady newcomer among our clientele. He was six feet tall weighing around 220 pounds, handsome you could say, with silver-gray hair and a heavy military mustache. He didn't do much but sit at a table by himself and listen to us play. I thought maybe it was my imagination, but he seemed to show a lot of interest in my act.

One night he called a waiter and said to bring him half a dozen ham and egg sandwiches. The way Tait's made ham and egg sandwiches, one was a meal.

I DIDN'T MAKE A MILLION

"You want half a dozen sandwiches?"

"Yes."

"Well, that's what you'll get."

Was he astonished when the waiter lined them up! I couldn't help laughing, and he beckoned me over.

"That's not the way we serve them in Shanghai. We order one but it comes cut up in six pieces, so we say half a dozen. Son, sit down. Help me out on these. I'm like a native in a strange country."

We talked. He told me his name was Louis Ladow and he was the owner of the Old Carlton Cafe in Shanghai. I didn't know it at the time, but the Carlton was world-famous among people who traveled. Mr. Ladow told me he had gone to China as a steward on a liner in the old days. He left the ship and went into business. He opened the Carlton Hotel in an old wooden building in the heart of the commercial district on Ningpo Road. To begin with it was a small restaurant downstairs with a few rooms on the second floor. Later he remodeled the upstairs into the Old Carlton.

"Look, son, I've been watching you work here. How would you like to come to Shanghai and work for me?"

Just like that. He proceeded to offer me a year's contract, complete with passage over and back. Just like that I said I'd take it. At the moment, for all I cared, they could turn Tait's and the Little Club into a coffee shop and restaurant any time they wanted. Whitey Smith was headed for China!

One trouble with me, I suppose, is over-enthusiasm. When something looks good I go for it, head over heels. I decide first and think about the consequences afterwards. If things go sour I pull out. Mr. Ladow's proposition did give me a couple of thoughts the next few days. Just how do you pull out of China if things go wrong? Shanghai is about five thousand miles

WHITEY SMITH

from San Francisco and in those days it took the better part of a month to cross the Pacific. Besides there is always a war on over there somewhere and a guy might get shot. But there was the guaranteed return passage. Mr. Ladow looked like a straight shooter. And speaking of straight shooting we heard the Chinese weren't very good marksmen, and I could run fast.

Then again there was the problem of my best girl. Florence and I were very much in love and I couldn't see leaving her behind while I poked around among the night clubs in Shanghai. She liked night life too.

Leaving my folks was no real problem since I had been on my own for some time, but the idea of it tugged at the heartstrings. Papa and Mama Schmidt (Schmidt is the name I was born with – Sven Eric Heinrich Schmidt) lived in Oakland across the bay from San Francisco. My dad was an immigrant from Denmark, and in fact so was I. Sea travel was not new to me but the voyage to America happened so long ago I couldn't remember much of it.

My dad had a tough time putting enough meat and potatoes on our table in the little Danish town of Vejle where I was born, so he decided to take off for the land of milk and honey, America. He was a cabinet maker and a good one, so it didn't take him long to get a fairly good job in San Francisco. I still don't know why he went all the way from Ellis Island to the West Coast but he did, and must have made pretty good money for a fellow who couldn't speak English. In 1906 he sent for my mother, two brothers and me. For the past year or so he had been mailing us the Sunday funny papers and from them my brothers and I had been trying to learn a little bit of English. When we left for the States with a twenty or thirty-word vocabulary we thought we knew all there was to know about the language.

The ship we sailed on from Copenhagen was nothing to write

about. I don't even remember her name. We were deep down in the hold, steerage passengers on a third class vessel. But we were so happy about the prospects for the future in a country where everybody had lots of everything, that the three weeks' crossing did not dampen our spirits. The authorities at Ellis Island were kind to us and before we could get used to being on firm ground again we were on the streets of New York City. That's where I saw my first negro. My brothers and I turned and ran like hell in the opposite direction. Mother got an Irish cop to catch us and bring us back. The old colored gentleman said, "Young fellows, why you afraid of me? I's your friend. I'd like to shake hands with you boys."

The Irish cop put our hands into his and that was our introduction to wonderful America.

2

THE IRISH COP helped us get to the railroad station. Mother had a heck of a time buying tickets for San Francisco with the money papa had sent. She hadn't even learned English from the funny papers. She knew one word – "hamburger". By the time we got to the West Coast I wished she had learned another word. At every meal stop we ate nothing but hamburgers.

Mama Schmidt would bundle us out of a train into a depot restaurant, (they didn't have diners for people like us in those days) carrying all the belongings we had for fear somebody would steal them if we left them aboard. People would smile at the major production we made of getting settled around a table. Mama would cross her hands on her lap, look the waiter in the eye and say "Ham-o-or-ghers". Then he would say something and Mom would say hamburgers again while we all stared at him. After a while he would go into the kitchen and bring back hamburgers. Paying the checks when we finished eating was like burning the mortgage with all the clan gathered around for the ceremony.

At one station, while we were eating our third or fourth hamburger for the day, a train pulled in on the track between the station and our train. Mama Schmidt was too busy to notice this, but she did notice when the newly arrived train began to pull out. Of course she thought it was ours. She grabbed us all and our baggage, our mouths full of hamburger, and away we went. The four of us were strung down the track like laundry on a line

I DIDN'T MAKE A MILLION

shouting "Stop, stop!" – in Danish.

Mama Schmidt was a big woman but she could move fast. She hit her best Jesse Owens stride, skirts flapping like Fourth of July bunting. But she lost out to the machine age and had to give up. When we turned around, positive we had been left in a strange city practically broke, we saw a waiter with a mustache running down the track toward us waving the check we had failed to pay. There was a first class fuss when he caught up. In her best country Danish Mama Schmidt raised holy ned about trains pulling out without their passengers, especially us. The waiter was giving her both barrels, probably about people who ran out of restaurants without paying their bills. I remember and still laugh how they both talked at the same time, Mama with her hands on her hips and with frequent wild gestures, the waiter holding our check in one hand and striking it over and over with the palm of the other hand.

We got back to the station prepared to throw in the towel. Then we recognized our train standing where we had left it, just getting the all abo-o-ard signal. Mama Schmidt was kind of quiet when she paid the waiter. From there on to San Francisco things went pretty smooth. Some Chinese fellow was selling bananas and peanuts and Mama bought some. It was a welcome relief from hamburgers. It was the first time we had seen a banana, and as far as I was concerned they tasted like soap.

It must have been in the month of March when we reached San Francisco. We were in for a shock when we got off the train. Papa Schmidt wasn't there to greet us. We felt pretty lost, and I can remember panic as we stood there waiting for something to happen. Papa finally showed up and there were tears in his eyes as he picked us boys up one by one. He had been celebrating our arrival and had forgotten about the time. After three weeks in the hold of a third class steamer and ten days on the train with nothing but hamburgers, that lapse of memory seemed to make Mama Schmidt angry. She stalked out of the station to lead the family as she always did, but she had to come back because she didn't know where to go.

Papa Schmidt's failure was forgotten when we boarded our first cable car going up Market Street. I loved America right then. Papa had prepared well. We had a nice house on the corner of Van Ness Avenue and Vallejo Street. It was a whole lot better than we had been used to in Denmark and even Mama admitted Papa had done a pretty good job. Mama Schmidt and Papa Schmidt and all the little Schmidts were very happy people.

In those surroundings we were happy for about one month. Folks in our neighborhood were nice and friendly to us and the corner grocer even' gave us a little black mongrel dog which we called Prince. Prince liked the whole family but he liked Papa Schmidt best of all and wanted to be with him whenever he could. One Sunday morning he tried to follow Papa through a pair of swinging doors. He zigged when he should have zagged and one paw got caught. He made a heck of a fuss and with good reason because he dragged a back foot for the rest of his life.

Everybody remembers what happened in San Francisco at five o'clock in the morning on April 18, 1906. The Schmidt family had never experienced an earthquake before and we thought the world had come to an end. Like thousands of others we found ourselves running around in our nightclothes trying to figure what was happening to us. We could see outdoors at first but then we couldn't. It became pitch dark. Our house sank right down into the ground with only the tops of the windows showing from the street.

The fire department and the police came to our rescue after a while and dragged us through an opening in the top of the house, together with what household things we could scrounge.

I DIDN'T MAKE A MILLION

They left us to rescue other people and we took our meager salvage up on top of Telegraph Hill, from where we could see fires beginning to break out all over the city. Up there somebody in charge told us we would have to go to Oakland, but we would have to leave our belongings. No room on the ferry boat. So the Schmidt family started for the Ferry Building leading our dog Prince by a rope around his neck.

On the way some soldiers who were trying to keep people in line told us they had orders to shoot all looters and dogs, in that order. In other words we could not take Prince to Oakland. It was either turn Prince loose or have him shot, so we untied the rope and let the little mutt go, thinking we would never see him again. We three boys were all crying when we boarded the crowded ferry.

We got to Oakland all right and somebody, I don't know who, took charge of us. They took us to a district called Watts Track, near Emeryville. Once there we were bundled down to a place called Swede Alley, so called because mostly Scandinavians lived there. At least all the family was alive and we were together.

Two or three weeks later Papa Schmidt went back to Telegraph Hill to see what belongings, if any, were left.

What he saw brought tears to our eyes when he described it to us. There was our scrawny, half-starved little lame Prince standing on top of our pile of household goods, barking his heart out. Everything was there just as we had left it. The folks around there told Papa that Prince hadn't let anybody near our stuff, and the only thing he had to eat all the time we were gone was what Mama Schmidt had left there – two dozen raw eggs and a small box of chocolate candy.

Years later when Prince died our little black mongrel was given a war veteran's funeral and my brother Carl planted a cherry tree over his grave in our Oakland back yard.

3

Louis Ladow left San Francisco for Shanghai the next day after our conversation at Tait's about a contract. He had told me it was his last night in town. "You'll hear from me," he promised.

That was all I had to go on, so I made the most of it. I dreamed about Shanghai, talked about it, was sure I was going to make a million dollars in that fabulous city on the China coast.

When people began to take me seriously word got back to Rube Wolf, manager of the Little Club. Rube offered me five dollars more a week to forget about China. I said no soap and kept on talking and dreaming.

As the days dragged along I began to have my own doubts. Hell, Mr. Ladow had picked me for a musician and he didn't even ask me if I had a musical education. All he had to go on was sight and sound. As a matter of fact my education in music was pretty sketchy. Mama and Papa Schmidt decided one day I should augment my grade school lessons with taking piano on the side. They went to a lot of trouble digging up a piano for me and after several months of da-da-de-de-do up the scale of C they became pretty discouraged with little Sven Eric.

One night at the supper table I was drumming with my knife and fork and a brilliant idea came to Papa Schmidt. He reasoned that since anything would be an improvement over my piano playing I had been wasting time on the wrong instrument. It was obvious that I was a natural drummer.

So the next Sunday he took the family to a picnic at Shellmont

I DIDN'T MAKE A MILLION

Park not far from where we lived. The bandstand was right next to the bar where the musicians gravitated during the intermission. Papa graduated there too and took me with him. It didn't take long to get acquainted with Bill Nolding, the band's drummer. A few beers between Papa and Bill and I was set to go the next Sunday morning to Brother Nolding's house.

Of course he discovered right away that I really was a "natural drummer" since he was the one giving the lessons. Papa Schmidt, sure that I would someday play a drum concert for the King of Denmark, took his last sixty-five dollars over and above his beer money to buy me a set of drums.

Daily I sat before our old wind-up gramaphone drumming to beat the band, originating my own beats and, being a ham, learning the technique of juggling the sticks. I was even hired to drum now and then for certain auspicious occasions.

I remember one time I was hired to participate in the payoff ceremony of a famous heavyweight fight. Two of the elders in the Watts Track district of Oakland were loud in support of their respective choices to win the Johnson-Jeffries bout. They were not exactly sober when they agreed on the terms of the bet. The loser was to push the winner in a wheelbarrow two miles on Sunday morning to the ball park and return, and buy all the beer the winner could drink, both going and coming. I was hired, for one dollar, to walk behind the wheelbarrow and drum.

We drew a crowd that increased at each bar we passed. By the time we got to the ball park neither the pusher nor the sitter knew whether it was a ball game or a bull fight. On the way back the winner couldn't get out of the wheelbarrow, so they brought his beer out to him. By the time they got back to the starting point he couldn't even lift a beer, so the loser decided to deliver him to his home. That was a big mistake. His wife was waiting on the front porch with their youngest in her arms. She set the

WHITEY SMITH

child down, went into the house and came back with a bucket of water which she threw all over her husband, the pusher of the wheelbarrow, and me. I didn't even get my dollar but I did get blisters with all that drumming and walking.

There were other jobs I promoted as a drummer which were more profitable and less tiring. I made a proposition one day to the owner of the Mint Saloon in Oakland, on the corner of 10th and Broadway, to play from five to seven on Saturday nights when the shipyard workers would be cashing their weekly pay checks over the bar. He said he would give me the job if I would find a piano player to go along with me. Our pay would be two dollars apiece per night and the privilege of passing the hat.

I remembered hearing a newspaper man playing the piano one night at a religious meeting I was watching from the side lines. This fellow had one leg missing from above the knee and he walked on crutches. After I was sure he had a hat, I talked the proposition over with him and we teamed up. It worked pretty good. When it came time to pass the hat I would take his crutches and slip out and hide them and he would hop up and down in the front of the bar with his hat in his hand. We didn't last many weeks, but while we did we collected quite a few nickels and dimes and once in a while some quarters.

Jazz was just beginning to get a toe hold and I got a head start on what was later to be popular. Next, I teamed up with the district dog catcher who played the accordion and we booked ourselves for five dollars apiece at picnics, lunch rides, and the like. Besides the fiver, we got all we could eat and drink and when somebody stood up his girl it was either the dog catcher or Sven Schmidt who came to the poor damsel's rescue.

I couldn't stand prosperity though. I had money in my pocket and a reasonably full belly. Along with my music I was earning occasional dough as a professional fighter, bantam class.

I DIDN'T MAKE A MILLION

Whiskers were beginning to sprout on my cheeks and I knew just about everything there was to know about everything. In fact, I was so smart and so successful that I began to stay away from home for extended periods. Papa Schmidt took a dim view of this and finally laid down the law. So I took my ties and socks and my one suit, along with my drums, and went over the back fence when Papa wasn't looking.

It took about a month after I left home to become very hungry and very broke. Somehow the dog catcher and I didn't book so many jobs and it took more money to live when the folks weren't footing the home bills. It took a long time and lots of ups and downs, from selling newspapers to taking some fine beatings in the prize ring before I finally got a steady job playing at 'The Loge" owned by Jack Perkins. I bought some clothes and ate three squares a day. I drummed every night and began developing innovations in my style and learning new songs.

Soon I was asked to play in bigger and better places, even with combos and small bands. I had originated a drum outfit that was the envy of all the drummers in the area. It was a big, square nickel-plated rack with little colored lights all around the top that blinked off and on. I hung everything imaginable on it that had a tone, such as a small frying pan, sleigh bells, tomtoms, cowbells, a small chamber pot and, for looks only, a stuffed monkey on a trapeze. I sat in the middle of this monstrosity and did tricks in syncopation. Whitey had more fun than anybody, but the customers seemed to like it too.

4

SHANGHAI WAS NOT JUST a dream inspired by Louis Ladow. One day I got word to show up at the office of the China Mail Line. There would be a ticket waiting for me. I don't remember how I got there but it must have been a record for speed.

There was not only one ticket waiting for me but two tickets, with some instructions from Mr. Ladow. Among the instructions was a piece of advice. I had mentioned that night in Tait's that I was going to have a heck of a time leaving Florence behind. I had been going with her off and on since 1916, and the last year or so we were practically engaged.

The advice from Mr. Ladow was to the effect that Shanghai was a wicked city and a fellow was better off married than single. So Florence became Mrs. Whitey Smith and on the 24th of August,.1922, we boarded the old s.s. Nile of the China Mail Line, a vessel of perhaps three or four thousand tons, and sailed westward through the Golden Gate.

As a parting inducement, Rube Wolf had offered me ten dollars more a week if I would continue to play for the Little Club. "Boy," he said, "you don't want to be taking off for that heathen country. I hear they got a war on over there all the time. It ain't safe."

How right he was, and how little we cared at the time. We were off for China!

Aboard with us was a fiddle player Mr. Ladow had picked up to play at the Carlton. I remember him as Benny. Also the president of the China Mail Line, an old Chinese gentleman by the name of Mr. Chen, I think it was. He and his family were going back to the homeland to retire.

We made a stop at Honolulu in the Hawaiian Islands, then on to Yokohama and Kobe in Japan. The most interesting stop on the trip was the next Japanese port, Nagasaki. The good ship Nile had to refuel there.

The Nile was a coal burner. Refueling was done the hard way from barges alongside by means of a human chain of Japanese women, children, old and young men carrying baskets. They crawled up the side of the ship on a rope ladder. They dumped their baskets and crawled back down again to the barge on another rope ladder. I thought the moving chain looked like a huge black python on the prowl for a drink of water.

Mr. Chen told me each link in the human chain got fifteen cents a day, working from early morning until dark. It was my first astonishing impression of Oriental labor.

The operation was very dirty. By the time we pulled anchor for Shanghai the passengers were almost as black-faced as the Japanese who carried coal.

The Nile's skipper, Captain Kinley, took an erratic course for Shanghai. He told me they were dodging around trying to escape a typhoon. We hit some rough weather but on September 14th we steamed up the Woosung River into Shanghai harbor, tying up at the Merchants Wharf.

My great adventure was opening out before me and I felt like an awe-struck, happy kid. Mr. Ladow had found out somehow that this was the date I was born and as we walked down the gangplank an American band was playing Happy Birthday. Right then I knew I was going to like Shanghai, just as sixteen years before I fell in love with San Francisco when Papa Schmidt took us on a cable car up Market Street.

WHITEY SMITH

I wish I had the words to describe Shanghai as it was then, a great sprawling colorful stately city of contrasts with a fascination of its own. There never was anything like Shanghai in its prime, and I guess there never will be again. Years later I picked up a book written by a famous woman doctor of Shanghai, Dr. Anne Walter Fearn, who became my good friend. Dr. Fearn had a couple of paragraphs in her little privately printed uncopyrighted book that recalled Shanghai exactly as it appeared to me that first day.

She said it was here that East met West in a jumble of cooperation, misunderstanding, struggle and friendship. She wrote that Shanghai was a city of hustling, bustling, hurrying, jostling millions. It was a city of noise and confusion. Tramcars clanged their gongs, motor cars tooted their horns, coolies sing-songed as they trudged under great burdens, "ah yee-ah yee."

Chinese men walked the streets dressed in long silk gowns, blue cotton ones or in the latest Western styles. Some Chinese women were beautifully gowned with smart waved hair, sideslit skirts, silk stockings and high-heeled shoes. Some wore the divided skirts and embroidered jackets of tradition. There were Japanese, Indians, Americans, Annamese and Europeans, a conglomeration of every nationality under the sun.

She described the traffic in all its varieties – pedestrians, rickshaws, handcarts, wheelbarrows, bicycles, motor cars, buses and trains. Occasionally a passage had to be cleared for a patrol of mounted Sikhs on shining groomed horses, carrying lances from whose tips floated red and white pennants. They would be on their way to head some parade. And the crowds of Chinese, not only moving about the streets but silent, gaping crowds, obstructing every moving thing.

That was the way it looked to us, too. Our first night in China made us feel like Hollywood celebrities. The gang at the Carlton dined us, wined us and treated us as though we were the greatest

I DIDN'T MAKE A MILLION

thing that ever happened to Shanghai in years.

The Old Carlton was a ramshackle two-story building by day. By night it had glamor. The Chinese hadn't learned to dance Western style yet so the clientele was strictly foreign, composed of a society known in Shanghai as the "International 400". I suppose it was as select a crowd as you would have met anywhere in the world at the time, at least in a night club. Nowhere, I am sure, would you find more beautiful or better-dressed women.

September is still summer in that part of China. The climate is hot and humid. At the Old Carlton I saw the first air conditioning I had ever seen in my life and probably the first ever seen in Asia. Of course it is nothing like the sleek and efficient air-cooling devices that came along later, but it kept folks reasonably cool while dancing.

The system was ingeniously composed of a three-foot picket fence in the middle of the dance floor surrounding a dozen or more large blocks of ice. A large but quiet ceiling fan whirled smoothly overhead, distributing the ice-cooled air out around the dance floor. The waiters had strung blue and green colored lights among the blocks and around the fence.

It was a fine place to play and I was happy and prosperous. Benny the fiddler who came with us didn't stay long, as when I arrived there were already six men in the band. We worked well together and some time later I was made leader. I made many changes, importing some new musicians, mostly from San Francisco.

Louis Ladow was a big operator and he foresaw big things for the future. In order to be prepared for more and better business he promoted what he planned to call the New Carlton. In fact he was in the States buying things for it when I first met him. It was in the process of building when I arrived.

In December of 1922 it was finished. The New Carlton

was located across the street from the Shanghai Race Track on Bubbling Well Road. It was a mammoth thing, beautifully appointed and many years ahead of its time. Inside was a huge night club. Adjoining it on the Nanking Road side was a super-plush dining room. Adjoining that was the Carlton movie theater.

The whole set-up was far out of proportion to the available business of that time. Its patrons were foreigners, for the Chinese had not learned to dance and hadn't acquired the night club habit. Competition for the foreign trade was heavy. I believe there were more night clubs in the International Settlement of Shanghai at that period and subsequently than in any other city of comparable size in the world.

We opened with a tremendous show and wore our hearts out to make the New Carlton a success. But the International 400 simply couldn't support the overhead and it wasn't long before Mr. Ladow knew that he had miscalculated.

He had many friends in Shanghai and they helped with their patronage and in other ways as much as they could. Many old residents remembered and showed outstanding gestures of generosity at the outbreak of the first World War. The Old

Carlton was always generous with credit and when a large number of younger men in Shanghai were called up for service, all patrons of the Carlton, they couldn't pay several months of back chits.

On the morning of the sailing, Mr. Ladow appeared at the Customs jetty with a huge crowd gathered to see the men off to war. He had his pockets stuffed with chits and began tearing them up in the presence of the crowd, waving goodbye and shouting "We're all even, fellows! Hurry back and start all over again!"

When the New Carlton failed and closed, it not only broke Mr. Ladow financially but it broke up his family and in the end broke

I DIDN'T MAKE A MILLION

his heart. He died in the arms of an old friend, Obie O'Brien.

5

NOW I HAD PROBLEMS. The New Carlton was gone and our jobs with it. I had a first class dance band on my hands and no money to pay salaries. But Providence was with me this time. Hongkong & Shanghai Hotels, Limited, controlled the top-level hotel business throughout China. They were a really big and stable outfit. When they offered me and my band a job playing in the Peacock Grill Room at the Astor House in Shanghai we didn't waste any time accepting it, we jumped at it.

I sent to the United States for six new American musicians and on November 20, 1923, fourteen months after I arrived in China, my new band and I opened with a bang and from that day on we played to capacity crowds.

But the Hongkong-Shanghai Hotels, like Mr. Ladow, were not satisfied and thought that they should have something bigger. So after careful consideration, they purchased the George McBain mansion which took in a full square block of Bubbling Well at the corner of Seymore Road. Poor Brother McBain practically had been camping out with only thirtyone suites. The setting was like paradise with beautiful elaborate Chinese gardens surrounding the mansion.

My band and I kept making music for large well-paying crowds at the Astor House while they turned the McBain mansion into a new hotel with a three-million-dollar ballroom big enough to accommodate eighteen hundred people. Mr. James Taggert, the managing director, hired a famous French architect to deign what turned out to be, I can say without fear of contradiction, the most elaborate and grandest dance pavilion anywhere.

When I went over to look at it I couldn't believe my eyes. I was absolutely flabbergasted! The ballroom was goldleaf and marble in the shape of a four-leaf clover with a huge fountain in the middle. There were two-inch Peking carpets covering the table area. Murals and ceilings were done by famous artists of Italy and France. Off to one side of the ballroom was the Empire Room where only royalty could enter. For cocktails before dinner they had the Winter Garden, with running waterfalls, artificial stars in the "sky" which sported a traveling moon.

My first reaction was that this place was also years ahead of its time. I felt that they were making the same mistake that Mr. Ladow made. Who was going to support this big layout? The foreigners in Shanghai and the tourist trade certainly were not enough to pay off even the investment. I told Mr. Taggert that without doubt he had the world's most beautiful ballroom, but if China didn't learn to dance and begin to patronize us, he had just buried three million dollars. Mr. Taggert told me with a quick parry and thrust that was my responsibility.

I didn't know exactly how I was going to do it, but I knew that I had to have more people with money to spend to fill the tables on our two-inch thick Peking carpet. Obviously, I had to draw in the rich Chinese.

To appeal to the Chinese mind I was sure that I had to have something different. They would not be satisfied, I believed, with just good danceable music. I had to have something bizarre with plenty of novelties, Some of the things I tried in that beautiful gold-plated, marble pillared ballroom bordered on heresy. They resembled the Disney fantasies. I had a miniature train built to run round, over and through the band stand and Mama Schmidt's son, Whitey, stood out in front of the band swinging a red lantern calling out the names of Chinese stations while my musicians rendered choo-choo effects in the background.

There was a number called Kitten on the Keys which I thought was good. We built a tremendous black cat and stuffed it with old rugs and placed it on our grand piano. Spring-driven motors made it move like a playful Siamese while my piano player made like a tom cat on the ivories.

Another month and a few Chinese began to drop in for a look-see, but, of course, they didn't dance since they didn't know how. At the same time I had to keep our International 400 happy because they were the people who were spending the money which paid the overhead. There was still a large deficit. I didn't know what else to do but I knew I couldn't give up. If I did, there was no place to go except down, and I'd been that way once already.

I had a friend, a general in the Chinese Army whom we called General William. He was a graduate of Notre Dame and a regular patron of the Majestic. Because of his American background, he liked our music. General William and I became intermission pals and I told him about my problem. The Chinese general had an answer.

"Whitey", he said, "your music is good and I enjoy it. From what you tell me, you are trying to bring more Chinese into the Majestic ballroom."

I told him that he was so right.

"If you are going to do that, you are going to have to play music that these people understand. The Chinese ear," he continued, "is educated only for melody. You must get that modern deep harmony out of your music and stay more with the melody." I began to see his point.

How we struggled! The melody was there in the stuff we had been playing, but it was buried under crazy accents and trick harmony and the Chinese couldn't find it, or remember it.

We scouted around and found the music to some old Chinese folk song melodies adaptable to band treatment. Chinese music is scaled high. It is repetitious and sing-song. To the American or European ear it sounds like a rising and falling wail from a torture chamber. It is punctuated with clashing cymbals.

A couple of the boys assisted by interpreters worked out arrangements based on Chinese music with – to them – familiar melodies. The saxes, trombones or flutes carried the tune, the only variation being by octaves. Sometimes the violin would take over. Guitars and traps were worked into the background, softly.

Jimmy Elder was our piano player, and a good one. Poor Jimmy. He tried hard to work the piano in somehow, but pianos just don't fit Chinese music.   Nine trained fingers became useless. Only one was needed. It drove Jimmy nuts.

It was monotonous torture for all of us, but we stuck to it and more Chinese began to drift in. At first it was out of pure curiosity. Then they began to flock in for enjoyment.

Of course we didn't play Chinese music exclusively. We had to keep the International 400 happy too. We calmed down the Charleston and brought out the melody in it. We played Dardanella and the Missouri Waltz, Stumbling All Around, Somebody Loves Me, and Who. We alternated with our Chinese adaptations and gradually got something of a dance beat into them. The Duke of Kent, one night before a dinner party he was giving, brought me the music to five or six numbers which all became very popular.

The Chinese liked it and clamored for more. Before long they began to dance. They liked Singing in the Rain, Parade of the Wooden Soldiers, and the Doll Dance. Once in a while we would really let go with the St. Louis Blues and you could feel the younger Chinese begin to catch fire with it.

My friend General William was right. At Sunday afternoon dances, the Majestic ballroom began packing to capacity. eighteen hundred people. Many of the 400 were waiting on the outside to get in.

I shall always remember a compliment paid me by Pearl Buck, the famous writer who was herself an Old China Hand. She remarked to some of her friends that Whitey Smith had brought more good will to China than many an ambassador. He had taught China to dance. I give General William a great big hand for his timely assist on that one.

6

ABOUT THE TIME the Majestic ballroom was packing them in, there was a vest-pocket war known locally at the time as the Kiangsu-Chekiang trouble going on near Shanghai. There was some shooting in a little country village called Wuhu, not far outside the city.

My friend General William asked me if I would like to visit the front, and would I like to bring some friends. I told him sure, this should be very interesting, but how would we get up to the front lines. He said he would take care of that – if we really wanted to get that close.

Next day the General brought me a long paper covered with Chinese characters, decorated with a red seal and a blue ribbon. This was my pass to the war. I had reason to wish later that he hadn't been so generous with his passes.

Of course General William had a Chinese name, but I don't remember it. I don't even remember, if I ever knew, what army he belonged to or what his job was. All I recall is that he was associated with a young leader named Chiang Kai-shek. Chiang was not too well-known to me at the time. He was just another name in the confusing jumble of intriguers and fighting men in this "period of the war lords" of the middle 1920's.

Chiang was associated in turn with Dr. Sun Yat Sen's forces. Dr. Sun had succeeded in establishing himself in 1921 as the legal and constitutional President of the Chinese Republic. It was their object to unify the country and one of the main objectives at the time was the capture of Shanghai. Sun was having plenty of opposition from northern China. Also his own factional troubles with the Russians whom he had invited to help him launch his new Republic.

I gathered up some of the friends I'd made who, I thought, would be interested, among them a sprinkling of newspapermen who welcomed the chance to see some close-up action. We prepared to make the trip on the first rainy day. We chose a rainy day because we had heard that when it rained the Chinese warriors stopped fighting and got out their paper umbrellas until the weather moderated. I don't know where that canard got started. Must have been some newspaper correspondent's version of an old war, "covered" from a saloon. Anyhow it was still generally believed among Americans and it was enough for us.

Among those in the party were Russell Ellis, "Demon" Hyde, Jeff Anderson and Claude McGuire, all of them World War I veterans, as was Whitey Smith. Whitey never got overseas. That's another story which we can go into later. Also among us was a Spanish-American War veteran named Charley Hannigs. Charley would show you his wounds if you didn't believe him.

We got a car and a Chinese chauffeur and come the first rainy day we were off to the wars. Our only weapons were bottled goods, which proved effective. Every time we passed a sentry we had to show our pass, which, of course, called for another drink around. The veterans with me were getting braver by the minute, bragging loudly about their exploits in other wars. (What a laugh this war was if they didn't fight on rainy days.)

Before long we heard some boom-booms and ra-ta-ta-tas which increased in volume and frequency the nearer we got to the front. I didn't care much for this as the party was promoted by me and I felt some responsibility as well as, I must admit, genuine concern for my skin. We stopped for consultation and I broached the idea of turning around. I was voted down.

Before long we met a friend of mine, Al Meyer, editor of the Shanghai Evening News, who was on his way back from the front. Al said he had to crawl part of the way on his stomach. He was covered with mud, and in China this is something you don't want for dessert.

I had another try at getting the expedition turned in the proper direction but our brave heroes wouldn't listen and threatened to go on without me. We all had another drink and pressed ever onward. A short distance ahead we saw nothing but dead soldiers on both sides of the road and the boom-boomboom and the ra-ta-ta-ta were getting louder and louder. For a rainy day these Chinese were making a hell of a lot of noise.

It was time for common sense to step in, so I stepped out of the car and told my brave veteran friends that they could go on by themselves. I had no more than finished my declaration when a bullet hit the dirt right in the middle of our group. I was the first one back in the car, but all my ex-hero friends were lying on top of me. Our Chinese chauffeur somehow lost his Oriental calm and jammed the starter while the bullets were flying around us like corn in a popper.

Inside the car nobody moved. I was being squashed by the ex-heroes on top of me, so to keep from becoming liquidated by sheer weight I decided to take the easy way out. Between death rattles I suggested we get out and push the car. So what do they do? They pull me, Whitey Smith, from the bottom of the heap and push me out in the open to see if I would draw fire.

By some miracle, or perhaps for lack of ammunition, the firing stopped and I finally got my ex-hero war veterans to give me a hand pushing the car. Until we could safely turn it around and get the engine started, that automobile was pushed faster backwards than the motor had carried us toward the front.

When we got back to Shanghai we had nothing to show but souvenirs picked up from the dead on the way back, safely out of snipers' range. The newsmen got some photos for their papers and we all got a changed impression of the character of a Chinese war.

We wondered at the time where the Chinese got hold of all that ammunition they were shooting so freely. In view of the tricks that were played on them by smugglers and crooks, I still wonder.

Shanghai was full of smugglers and fast-buck men and in those days it was a paradise for their kind. There were dozens like the fellow we may as well call Percival, which was not his name. Percy was a newspaper man who arrived in 1925 and went to work on the China Press. He later became editor of it. He was the kind who would sit down and tell you with a straight face that he was the real composer of the Star Spangled Banner.

Well, Percy was always on the move. Finally he got in trouble with the owners of the paper. But before he was fired Percy had contacted some Chinese generals who needed rifles. Through his press connections he had heard about a shipment of arms arriving for the Shanghai Volunteer Corps.

Percy "borrowed" a white uniform and introduced himself as a United States Navy commander. He hired a big black sedan on which he hung the official U.S. Navy pennant and took the generals with him to the dock to watch the arms being unloaded.

Percy made a great show of walking up and down the rows of stacked crates marking certain ones with chalk. On these he collected a "deposit", pending delivery, of two hundred dollars per crate.

That night, when the Chinese generals came to collect their arms and pay the balance, the crates were all gone and Percy was

I DIDN'T MAKE A MILLION

on a freighter headed for the United States.

7

BACK IN THE OLD DAYS in Oakland I used to fancy myself as a fighter. With the passing years I outgrew a splendid opinion of myself, possibly because I had it knocked out of me.

It is a wonder that I didn't get into more trouble than I did in Shanghai. There was plenty of it around. Some very tough people inhabited the barrooms and cabarets. I remember one adventurous evening that almost put me back in the fight business, strictly in an amateur capacity. I will get to that a little later.

There was a tough gang in the neighborhood of Swede Alley in Oakland, where we lived after the earthquake. I had to fight my way along and many times I got my ears pinned back. So I did what to me was the obvious thing. I played hookey from school and spent my time, or a good deal of it, around the Oakland Athletic Club, where a lot of professional fighters were training.

My constant presence around the club finally attracted attention. The number one boxing instructor who was an ex-Australian featherweight champion by the name of Percy Cove asked me, "Sonny, why don't you go to school? Why are you always hanging around here?"

I told him I wanted to learn how to fight and he told me I couldn't have come to a better place. I was there for more than a year, doing odd jobs, punching the bag, skipping rope and working out on the sand bag. Percy wouldn't let me box with the bigger fellows, however, so I was never sure how much I knew.

I DIDN'T MAKE A MILLION

After I left home by way of the back fence, it didn't take long for me to become very hungry and very broke. The only job I could get was as a newsboy. I began selling newspapers at the corner of 12th Street and Broadway in Oakland.

The young toughs in the neighborhood, however, were not about to permit an invasion of their territory and it wasn't long before they were trying to run me off my corner. But I was hungry and had plenty of incentive to stay there. What Percy Cove taught me came in very handy. After one fight I found that I had licked the bantam champion of Oakland.

I thought in the first flush of victory that fighting for a living might be better than selling newspapers, so I made my way down to the office of the number one boxing promoter of that day. I boxed a few rounds for him and he said, "Young fellow you fight Friday night. Ten dollars if you win. Five dollars if you lose." Ten dollars, I thought. More money than I ever had at one time before.

The promoter asked "What is your name, Muscles?". I told him "Sven Eric". "What? You should raise a beard and become a fiddle player. As of now, you are Frankie Smith!"

The night of the fight I was sitting in Mead's Cafeteria on the corner of 7th and Broadway hoping somebody would stake me to a meal. The steward there knew me and had learned I was going to fight that night. He asked me if I would like something to eat.

"Yes, sir," I said, "I would like to have a piece of that strawberry pie."

With a little luck and in spite of the strawberry pie I won my first fight. With this I had my choice of managers. I chose Jack Perkins who was handling the then-famous "Oakland Frankie" Burns. Frankie had once fought Ad Wolgast for the lightweight championship of the world.

WHITEY SMITH

I fought a few oldtimers and then had my chance at the bantamweight title of Oakland. The holder was Joe Gorman, the fellow I had licked in a newsboy street fight. This was a big chance for me but the promoter told me I would have to change my name. Frankie Smith was all right but there were too many Frankies in the business – Frankie Edwards, Frankie Burns, Frankie Jones.

I took the problem to my newsboy buddies and we had a board of directors' meeting at the newsstand on Twelfth and Broadway. One of the "directors", brighter than the rest, looked at my blond hair and said "I got it! It's a natural. Whitey Smith!" And that's been my name ever since. Incidentally my brother Holger was called Whitey, too.

The fight with Joe Gorman was easy enough since I had already licked him once and had his number.

I could really say that boxing was bringing me my pork and beans, and now and then ham and eggs, but my manager got money-hungry and before long he had me matched with Eddie Miller, the bantam champ of California. They told me I was going to get fifty dollars for the fight, but they did not tell me that my manager was going to get seventy-five. It seemed to me that I was being pushed too fast. Eddie was a pretty salty fighter and had much more experience than I did. I figured that I was in for a licking and I thought best to play it so that I wouldn't get knocked around and punchy. I knew pretty much what I was going to do.

Our fight was scheduled as a semi-final on a card at the Dreamland Pavilion in San Francisco. A friend of mine named Moose Taussig was my opponent's manager and a great friend of the referee, Harry Foley. With odds like that, I knew darn well the referee would not stop the fight for being dull because in such a case Eddie Miller would not get his money nor would

Moose Taussig. Harry Foley wouldn't do a thing like that to a good friend like Moose.

I had it figured right. I went in the ring that night and waltzed through a back-pedaling contest. I would hit and hold, bicycle backwards, push and hold and maul. Referee Foley saw through the whole thing and he warned us over and over again that if we didn't mix it up he would throw us out and we wouldn't get our money. But I kept on waltzing and Harry didn't stop the fight. Of course, Eddie Miller was the winner.

After the bout, when my manager and I went to collect our money, the promoter asked, "Do you have any more like him in Oakland?"

"I think we have," replied Mr. Perkins.

"Well, keep them there!" said the promoter.

That ended my boxing career for a while.

I gave up fighting and worked at various jobs, one of which was a combination drummer, bartender, waiter and bouncer at a joint called The Chateaux in Richmond, just a few miles out of Oakland.

This spot was off the main road on top of a mountain. We had a negro cook who doubled on the piano and when we saw the lights of a car coming up the hill toward us he ran for the piano and I made a bee-line for the drums and started to play. When the guests got settled, I mixed their drinks while the cook tickled the keys. Then I gave him the food orders and I sang and juggled drum sticks while he prepared them. When we came back to the piano, I served the food and then the two of us played dinner music while they ate.

After a while business picked up and the owner, Mr. George Davis, hired a bartender, Danny Cramer. In time the three of us became fast buddies.

George and Danny suggested that I make a come-back in

boxing. This should be easy, they said, since I hadn't gone very far anyhow. It was against my better judgment, but I agreed, since George would be my manager and I liked him a lot. George didn't lose any time getting into town to talk to a promoter, Tommy Simpson. Before I knew what had happened, he matched me with Tony Freitas, a little San Leandro Portuguese, who had fought the best. I was to start training the next morning.

But I postponed it a day. The same thing happened the next day, so I postponed the training again. That nonsense went on until three days before the fight, and, of course, George was disgusted with me. Then I suggested that I just run the road in the mornings, to improve my endurance. George was glad to get me to do anything. But, unfortunately, the Chateaux was surrounded by mountains and it was easy to trot out of sight, sit down for an hour and smoke cigarettes then splash water on my face from a nearby creek so it would look like I was sweating, then trot back puffing like a steam engine.

The night before the come-back, I did go to bed early. But at three in the morning, George and Danny knocked on my door. "Hey, Whitey, come on and get dressed, join the party."

"Listen, fellows," I protested, "I've got to fight tonight."

"Ah, what are you worried about? You'll knock that Portuguese out in the first round."

That was all the encouragement I needed.

That night at seven o'clock George and Danny took me to the Saddle Rock Cafe where I could get a good big steak to give me strength. Danny said I'd be so strong and I'd tear that San Leandro Portuguese to pieces. I got the steak all right, and ate it, but the waiters were passing my table with bowls of strawberries, which are one of my more pronounced weaknesses. My eyes were following the waiters and George noticed it.

"Whitey, would you like to have some strawberries?" Who

was I to quibble with my manager? So I had strawberries in quantities that would have stuffed a refrigerator. When we got to the auditorium, I was so full I could hardly breathe. I had the fight all figured out. I'd stall for a few rounds and then give all in the last two. As I climbed into the ring I looked over in the other corner. Good gosh! I didn't know that I was fighting Hercules! But I resolved to rely on my strategy.

The bell rang. I waltzed out. Tony came tearing out and he was fighting like he didn't like me. All he was doing was hitting me in the strawberries, and I didn't know what the heck to do.

George and Danny were giving me orders, shouting from my corner, "Hit and hold. Run!"

Run? Run where? What was it Joe Louis said? "He may run, but he can't hide."

Then Tony shot a long straight right to the middle that almost went through me and I just stood in the center of the ring gasping. The referee stepped between us and asked me if I was sick. I couldn't answer him with my breath knocked out. He looked around and then quickly called a doctor from ringside.

The sawbones saw splatterings of red on the canvas. "Stop it!" he cried, "This man has a hemorrhage."

It was only a strawberry hemorrhage but they raised Tony's hand in victory and I did give up fighting for a career of music.

Getting back to Shanghai, I remember one "fight night" that the boys in the band will never forget. After working at the Majestic, several of us decided to make the rounds, hitting all the night spots we could make. In Shanghai, in those days, this was no small job. I believe that city had more night clubs and cabarets per square mile than any other in the world.

Jimmy Elder, the piano player, was with us, along with Jess Sommers, saxophone, Russell Ellis, guitarist, Jeff Anderson and a couple of others. The agreement was that we would take turns ordering, and drink whatever was set before us. What a night! We didn't miss a place that was open and, in Shanghai, nothing ever closed.

Just as it was turning daylight and we were thinking of getting out of whatever place we were in, the biggest Russian I ever saw walked over to the table looking for trouble. Not being able to think of anything else to start it with, he accused me of going around with his wife.

I couldn't have hit the floor with my hat, but right away I wanted to fight. As I stood up, my buddies crowded around and tried to talk me out of it, but all I could see was this big Bolshevik standing in front of me so I let my best one go, took it on the lam. I thought everything was settled, but then I saw Jimmy Elder stooping over and holding onto his mouth. When he straightened up two teeth were missing.

Poor Jimmy. I had connected not with the Russian but with my own piano player.

8

There was nothing slow about Shanghai night life and we were right in the middle of it, my band and I. We had our good times and our troubles, both personal and businesswise. The rate of moral casualties among young business people and foreign residents was high. Some of the large banks, oil companies and tobacco houses in the middle twenties kept books on it. They figured that twenty to forty per cent of young unmarried men they brought out and put to work would eventually become useless to them and have to be sent home in disgrace. There were many suicides both among men and women.

Musicians, as a lot, are among the zaniest people you can associate yourself with, and perhaps the hardest to handle. Besides trying to keep them out of jail and paying off their debts I was father confessor to the boys and their wives – especially the wives.

If the third saxophone player didn't come home to mama on our day off, the little lady was pounding on my door wanting to know why. And if the bull fiddle-player's wife found her beloved with a brand new White Russian girl from Harbin, I was the first to be asked, "Why did you let it happen, Whitey Smith?" and, "Where is my ticket to go home?" And when the trumpet player showed up plastered on a very important night, I had the problem of doing either without him or doing with him, which was even worse.

My band consisted of twelve Americans, mostly from San

WHITEY SMITH

Francisco, with one-year contracts. Some brought their wives and children, but with or without, their salaries ran from $400 a month up with room and board. I was the unofficial "fixer upper" in family quarrels. I was the best man at five different weddings and called to the morgue to identify three of my musicians' wives who killed themselves through despondency.

All you had to do to buy anything in Shanghai in those days was to sign your name. The pencil was a symbol of the city, and Honest John Chinaman would trust the devil himself. With such temptation and the sky as the limit, I had to set myself up as a one-man collection agency to keep the authorities from running half my band out of China.

My first saxophone player, Jess, was a comedian. It just came natural with him. He just couldn't help it. He had a funny face. But Jess always had trouble with women.

When he arrived in Shanghai he had a cute little trick with him whom he introduced to me as his wife, Dorothy. It wasn't long before her real husband in San Francisco threatened to come out and shoot Jess if he didn't send Dorothy back to him. So I sent her back. Now my featured horn tooter was on the loose, and it didn't take him long to tie up with a White Russian "Princess". For a while it looked like she was the girl. One night at the Majestic Hotel, who should hobble in on crutches, her leg in a plaster cast, but the little cutie from San Francisco. When she had arrived back home, her husband had told her, "Go back to the guy who stole you."

Jess took one look and leaped off the bandstand and ran out of the door. He refused to see her or even to talk to her.

Of course I had to be the fixer again. She cried on my shoulder and told me that in Japan, coming from a party on her way back to the ship, she had fallen out of a rickshaw and had broken her leg. She had brought Jess a box of new sax reeds and new neckties. Would I please give them to him?

Jess wouldn't even see the poor girl, so I arranged for her ticket back to California again, taking out so much monthly from his salary to pay for it.

Now the Russian Princess having tired of Jess gave him the air, so brother Jess simply went down the line of ten girls at the Farren show, then playing at the Majestic Hotel, and picked number seven to be his bride. I had to get out my striped pants and tails and silk hat and be best man. The champagne flowed freely but what was the difference? Jess had a pencil.

When this charmer had been married two years, his wife produced a fine baby girl for him. But that didn't hold Romeo down. He was out nightly Romeoing the field for new talent, so his better half left for parts unknown.

There was one young man in my band, a trumpet player from Boston, who couldn't live without the bottle. He was a fine-looking young fellow who wore horned-rimmed glasses like Harold Lloyd. He was a great horse-back rider, a graceful dancer and the girls were crazy about him. Of all my problems, this guy was the worst.

Nearly every day the trumpeter would ride all over Shanghai on a rented horse (which he signed for) stopping at one bar after the other. When I saw his horse tied up in front of a bar, I knew what I was in for that night on the bandstand. It was trying, but he was a heck of a good trumpet player when he was sober enough to hold the instrument.

One Saturday night as I was getting out of my car at the hotel entrance, I saw a horse tied by the steps. I had a hunch that this was going to be the last straw. When I got inside, bearing out my worst fears, I saw my trumpet player, dressed in riding breeches rubbing elbows at the bar with our high-priced formally-attired clientele. The Duke of Kent and Sir Victor Sasoon were there, if I remember right. My man was with one of the girls from the red light district. Unceremoniously I escorted the barroom jockey and his companion outside to his horse. She sat on the rumble seat with her arms around his middle and away they galloped.

A few days later our British Chief of Police in Shanghai sent for me. He told me that he had met this ruffian with the horn-rimmed glasses and curly hair who worked for me, drunk or sober, on Nanking Road. The ruffian hollered, "Get out of the way, you bastard, and let a good man through!" And then had the audacity to gallop on his way.

The Chief told me, "Mr. Whitey Smith, if you don't get that drunken bum out of Shanghai by tomorrow, I'm coming to the hotel and drag him off the bandstand and break his American neck." And he meant it.

The s.s. *Empress of Canada* was lying in the Woosung River and was due to sail the next morning. I bought a ticket, picked up the trumpeter and took him to the ship on a small boat I rented. He was too drunk to take care of his fare, so I thought I would put the ticket in his suitcase. When I opened it up, behold! What do I see? No clothing, not even a pair of socks, but twelve bottles of brandy. Bon voyage!

Jimmy Elder, the piano player, was one of the old-school entertainers and was very popular with Shanghai's Rotary and Lions Clubs. He donated his services once a week, playing the piano for their community singing. There were two things Jimmy would rather do than anything else and they were having a drink and playing the piano. Jimmy, at the end of each month, had "shroff scare". A shroff is a Chinese chit collector, and a chit is universal language in the East for an IOU, the thing you use a pencil on.

After accepting his services for years the Lions Club members wanted to do something for Jimmy. They called a special meeting to decide what would be best, a present or cash. They decided on a fine 21-jewel wrist watch, and on the day it was presented to him there were speeches expounding Jimmy's virtues. All the club members stood up and drank to "d-e-e-e-a-a-a-r-old Elder," singing, "For He's a Jolly Good Fellow", and then they presented him with the watch.

Jimmy was called upon to say something and as he spoke he had tears in his eyes. "Gentlemen," he said, "you don't know how much I need this. Thank you all for making this trip to the hock shop possible."

"Uncle Ben", the pawnbroker, got the watch and Jimmy spent the proceeds in one afternoon at the bar.

I told him, "Jimmy, take it easy." He told me not to worry, since he had made arrangements to borrow from the Community Chest. "The Rotary Club has guaranteed me," he said.

Jimmy passed away in Shanghai in 1938, but I'm sure he is laughing with me and doesn't mind my telling the story.

9

SOME OF THE BOYS in the band were members of the Shanghai Volunteer Corps whose rifles Percy undertook to sell. I, if you please, was a corporal, and the authorities had instructed me and my squad in our detail, which was to patrol sections of the foreign settlement when trouble comes up. From time to time when there was curfew or there was fighting in the city we went to work at the Majestic in our uniforms, stacking our rifles and helmets back of the bandstand.

During one siege when thousands of Communist students passed out handbills and were inciting riots, the Majestic closed for a while and the band and I moved over to the Astor House to play temporarily in the Peacock Room. It was packed every night, since the foreigners living there were afraid to go outside the compound.

One night, while I was leading the band, all decked out in my corporal's uniform, a soldier walked across the floor and headed directly for the bandstand. We were playing, as I remember, a popular march entitled Washington Rose. The soldier halted in front of me and I stopped the music. A hush descended on the crowd and everybody looked at us.

"Corporal Smith", the soldier said in a voice loud enough for everyone to hear, "Captain Baldwin orders you to report with your squad at headquarters immediately."

Volunteer headquarters was right across the Garden Bridge on the premises of the old Shanghai Rowing Club. I told my men to get their rifles and helmets and double-time it across the floor, fall in at the entrance of the hotel and wait for me. I could see that the crowd was getting hysterical.

"What has happened, Mr. Smith?"

"God bless you."

"May you return."

Everybody seemed to be talking at once.

At the hotel entrance I gave the orders, "Squad! Attention! Forward, march!" And away we went.

"Corporal Smith reports for duty, Sir," I said with all the military bearing I could muster. The captain told me to report to the top sergeant. The sergeant in turn detailed us to guard the latrines in the Rowing Club.

The people back at the Astor were in near panic by now and some of the Britishers had dashed home to prepare to be called to their regiment. Rumors were flying fast and heavy. The thing built up from a street incident to the invasion of Shanghai by the Japanese.

Now, I don't doubt the importance of toilet facilities and I know that a lot of untoward incidents have happened in such places. But I seriously doubted if it was important enough that night to conscript the highest paid musicians in China as guards for a bunch of stand-up trenches.

So when all the boys were at their stations I went back to the hotel and went to bed. I was Corporal, wasn't I?

In May, 1925, the Commies put on a real demonstration. Besides passing out handbills and starting riots, thousands of them stormed the Nanking Road police station trying to release jailed students. The police shot right into the crowd on orders of the Scotch sergeant, killing many. The Indian Sikh guards were arresting students right and left.

I was on my way home from work at the height of the

demonstration. This mad crowd was running past my car with clubs and stones, shouting in Chinese. I didn't know until I got in front of the police station what had happened. A British policeman came over to me and said, "Get out of here, you bloody fool, if you want to stay alive! Can't you hear them shouting, 'Kill the foreigners, kill the foreigners'?"

Believe me, I left in a hurry and, fortunately I wasn't hurt.

In 1927 we went through this same thing all over again. This time all the servants and workers went on strike with the same slogan, "Kill the foreigners!"

It was so bad that the trusted number one lobby boy at the Astor House was standing on a soap box on Nanking Road, shouting, "Go home, white faces!" He seemed to have forgotten in the excitement that he was depending for a living on those same white faces he was trying to send home.

But the Communists had done their job well. Martial law was declared and things looked pretty grim. The band and I had our fun out of it. We acted as waiters during meal time and really had a ball trying to please our high-toned guests who were paying thirty to fifty dollars a day to stay in the Astor House. After a week or so the Chinese boys came back to normal, but the Reds were still working. Twenty years later they took over all of China.

Speaking of the Volunteer Corps and their troubles, I am reminded of the Chinese military which played a large part in keeping order in Shanghai. High in the Chinese army was a Canadian by the name of Morris Cohen.

Recounting the story of his rise to flag rank in the Chinese military junta, the General told Dr. Fearn that at one time in Shanghai he had become a close friend of a certain merchant and thereby found himself involved with a group which was actively supporting the Chinese Revolution, designed to overthrow the Manchu Dynasty. His career really started though when he knocked out a thug who was robbing his Chinese merchant friend.

Dr. Sun Yat Sen heard about the prowess of Mr. Cohen and offered him a position as bodyguard during the doctor's tour of Canada and the United States. After that, when Dr. Sun Yat Sen became the first president of China, Mr. Morris Cohen, then thirty-three years old, was given the rank of Colonel to act as Security Officer. In this capacity he saved President Sun's life. On the latter's death, Morris was promoted to General and was known as Mah Kun, which was as close as most Chinese could get phonetically to Morris Cohen, Morris to his friends was known as Two-gun Cohen.

During the years 1925-1927 there was continued trouble in the city caused by strikes, riots and nearby local wars, and the name Chiang Kai-shek rose on everyone's lips as a hopeful star for peace.

At first, Chiang's name was linked with the dreaded name of Borodin, the Communist who started the rush from Canton, driving all foreigners ahead of him. But Chiang Kai-shek broke away from Borodin and turned officially against the Communists before their army reached Shanghai, which actually it never did.

China was electrified to hear that cupid had brought together Chiang Kai-shek and the beautiful Miss Soong Mei Ling, American-educated daughter of an outstanding Chinese Methodist minister.

The family included three sisters and a brother, T. V. Soong, China's financial wizard. The three daughters became Madame Sun Yat Sen, Madame H. H. Kung and Madame Chiang Kai-shek. At the time, they were the acknowledged leaders of the New Women of China and on many occasions their parties were held at the famous Majestic Hotel where they danced to my music.

On December first, 1927, Miss Soong and the Generalissimo

were married in a private religious ceremony in the Soong mansion on Seymore Road. Dr. David Uii, General Secretary of the Y.M.C.A., officiated. Afterward, they moved on to the public part of this double-feature at the Majestic Hotel where the wedding was held Chinese style.

This was the big show to which thirteen hundred guests were invited. Outside, surrounding the hotel, there were thousands of people crowding the streets, craning their necks for a look see at the proceedings. The bride was given in marriage by her brother, T. V. Soong. The best man was Chiang's chief secretary, Liu Chi Wen. Except for Whitey Smith's music playing, "Here Comes the Bride", the wedding was like other Chinese weddings I played, only on a grander scale. The setting was gorgeous, and the brocaded gowns which graced the occasion, the most beautiful I had ever seen.

In this ceremony, the most important part was the bowing. There was a life-sized portrait of Sun Yat Sen hanging over the platform in the center of the ballroom. The bride and groom bowed three times to this enlarged picture, which was draped with the Nationalist and Kuomintang flags. Then the marriage certificate was read aloud and sealed. The bride and groom bowed to each other, once to the official witnesses, and once to the guests. Then the waiters started serving tea and we played, I'll be Loving You Always.

The General looked sharp in his foreign get-up of tails, striped pants and wing collar, but he didn't seem to be comfortable in this strange outfit. Madame Chiang wore the conventional foreign-style white satin and lace, and carried an immense bouquet. After the wedding, they left for their honeymoon in Chekiang, Hangchow, and Mokanshan, which were towns in General Chiang's home province. Upon their departure from the Majestic ballroom, we played for the Generalissimo and his bride, A Love Nest For Two.

Later I attended one of Madame's New Women of China parties. During dinner I sat by an old Chinese Mandarin from Soochow. At this time dairy products in China were used only to a very limited extent, and cheese and butter were not widely known or appreciated. The venerable old Mandarin helped himself to a dainty little butterball, slipping his long fingernail under it, and holding it up to his nose. He took a big whiff of its pungent smell and with a shiver slapped it back on the dish shouting, "Chi Mien! Smells like cow!"

In later years the Chinese started to dine more with the foreigners and ate Western foods with perfect table manners; and the foreigners in turn were dining with their oriental hosts and eating Chinese chow. At first we had a hard time manipulating the chopsticks which were placed before us, but soon we were experts.

10

My "military" experiences in the Shanghai Volunteer Corps actually reminded me of my hitch in the U. S. Army back in the old World War I days. I clowned my way through that one and never did get overseas. I might have done better if I had gone into the Marines with Paul Ash or the Navy with Paul Whiteman, but I don't think so.

Paul Ash was a well-known band leader on the West Coast at that time, with quite a reputation which later he built into a national one. He had long, wavy brown hair which was his trade mark, and an imagination which certainly would not have been an asset in any other business, because it was too screwball. In the night club music world it would have made him a fortune if he hadn't spent it as fast as he made it.

I was playing in a club in Oakland when one night Paul Ash dropped in for a night cap before taking one of his girl friends home. He listened for a while and told one of the waiters, "Tell that little squirt on the drums I will be back and talk to him tomorrow night."

When the waiter told me I darn near turned flipflops. Was he going to offer me a job? I walked on air.

Paul did come around the next night and offered me a job in San Francisco at fifty-five dollars a week. I was making thirty-five at the time. I would have accepted if he had asked me to play for nothing. Ash was my boy.

I moved my drums over to the Nurenberg, a German beer

garden in San Francisco, and found a new sign out in front that said "Come and See and Hear the Two Rag-o-Maniacs of Music Go Crazy". One of the rag-o-maniacs was supposed to be me.

The only thing wrong was that Paul didn't show for the opening night. He sent word that he was getting married, and for me to go screwball on my own. It wasn't easy since I had no idea what he wanted, but they didn't fire me. The next night Paul Ash showed up and we wowed 'em.

Three weeks later Sid Grauman heard us and asked Paul and me to book into his Strand Theater on Market Street. He had twenty-two piece string band and we were to be featured at eighty-five dollars a week. This would be a cinch, Paul said, because we had to go nuts only four times a day. But what they didn't tell us was that we had to provide the music for the movies, which were silent in those days. I stood it for one month. Paul quit too but soon looked me up again.

"Whitey, this time it's a dance hall. Ninety dollars a week and you work only four hours a day."

What he didn't tell me was that we played twenty-two dances an hour. But we had a fine band and we were popular. The First World War had started and business was better than ever.

Soon the word comes that Paul Whiteman, who had his band at the Fairmont Hotel, had enlisted in the Navy as a bandleader. He had his eye on me for a rate if I wanted to come along. I thought it over, but decided to stay where I was.

A short time later Paul Ash enlisted in the Marines as a bandleader and told me if I would come along he would try to get me a rate of sergeant. I guess they all wanted drummers.

I said no soap, Paul – I'd wait. A few months later I received a letter that stared up at me and said, "Greetings." Right then and there I was in the Army as Private Sven Eric Heinrich Schmidt. Drafted!

WHITEY SMITH

It didn't take the Army long to get me to Camp Lewis near Tacoma, Washington. When we arrived we had roll call and right away my troubles started. When the sergeant came to my name he stopped and apparently was spelling it out and then he said in the sarcastic tone that only a top kick can muster, "What do you know, men, we've got a heinie in the company. Listen to this – 'Sven Eric Heinrich Schmidt.' Ain't that just ducky?"

There were a couple of hundred eyes on this "heinie" and I didn't feel what you would call confident. Most of the men in that 13th Division were from Wyoming and Nebraska, wiry, sun-browned cowboys and ranchers not prone to feel real friendly toward anybody named Schmidt in their midst. After roll call I asked the fellow who looked as if he were in charge of our particular unit to take me to the captain, and after telling my story the captain said, "Yes, son, I know all about it. We broke that sergeant." He agreed that I should be transferred to another outfit.

Next thing I knew I was in "H" Company of the 76th Infantry Division and now I was with a bunch of sheep herders from Montana. I found out that applying the term "sheepherder" to people from Montana is neither correct nor wise.

We were told that for the first month we would be in quarantine, forbidden to leave not only the camp but our area as well. Each day started at six o'clock with drill, which kept up until five o'clock in the afternoon. After that we had five or ten minutes free time, some slum-gullion chow, then an hour or two of "why I hate the Army" and to bed. I missed my band, my soft bed, and especially my hundred and ten a week (I had been getting that after Paul left.) In other words, I was a little homesick, so I reported to sick call telling them that it was my stomach.

The doctor asked me if by any chance I thought that the

food might be causing my trouble. I kind of hedged on that one, saying yes, no, maybe – kind of gold bricking. When I got back to the company area that day the biggest sergeant I had laid eyes on told me that the captain would like to see me in the orderly room. When I got there the old Man said, "Sergeant, can't you make Pvt. Schmidt happy? This rookie here can't eat our food. Do something for Private Schmidt to make him happy."

It was nearly noon and the bugler sounded mess call. The sergeant ordered me to wait just outside the mess hall until he came to get me. A quarter of an hour later he led me to the door and then stopped short.

"Attention!!" He sounded like a Sousaphone and every man popped-to before his place.

The sergeant marched me up and down through each aisle like an inspection until we came to a special table set resplendent with white tablecloth, polished silver and flowers in a tin cup. A soldier strummed a ukelele and hummed softly close by. The sergeant bellowed, "Halt!" He pulled my chair out and said sit.

He gave the order "at ease" and a waiter in a white mess jacket handed me a menu.

I ordered pie and ice cream because I knew that it had to be purchased at the post exchange across the way from the barracks. Then I told him I would like some ham and eggs. I asked the ukelele player to play a couple of popular songs and took my time eating a leisurely meal. When I finished I laid a fifty-cent tip on the table, nodded politely to the big sergeant and hurried back to the orderly room and asked the captain for a transfer to the band at Division Headquarters right across the road. The captain made the necessary arrangements and there I was, a drummer once again.

Before long I had a small jazz combo organized, playing dates at the Red Cross canteen and the officer's parties. Or doing K.P.

WHITEY SMITH

I had no interest in anything but music and any time that I heard that the top kicker was winding up a detail for something called labor, I kept myself scarce.

One morning I made a mistake. When I should have come around the back door into our barracks I took the front road passing the platform where the sergeant was calling out a list of names to clean out the stables for the mules.

He noticed Sven Eric and he started shouting – hey, Schmidt – hey, Schmidt! I ducked into the door of our barracks. I could still hear the character shouting Schmidt at the top of his voice.

It wasn't long before I was told to report to the orderly room. As I stood at attention, the Topper asked me if I was hard of hearing. I told him that I was music deaf in my left ear. He stood up and said "Turn your right ear this way," and he screamed at the top of his voice.

"Two weeks K.P.! You heard that didn't you?"

Well, I worked that first day but I was trying to figure out a way to outsmart the guy with all this power over me. I'd noticed an old American Indian loafing around the camp. I found out that he was on sick leave. I offered him two dollars a day to register and do my kitchen police work. Everything worked out just dandy. All I had to do now was just keep out of sight. So, I made the hostess house my hangout where I had my meals and read magazines all day – oh boy! Did I put one over!

Some time later, we were on a march miles out to the Rifle Range for our monthly rifle practice. After that long hike with a heavy pack the top kicker details me to operate one of the targets. I had to pull this baloney up and down, pointing to the hit and miss. That wasn't so bad (but it started raining like heck) and the shooting ceased. There was a lull. I sat there waiting for some action but it kept on raining so I figured that they had left for home and forgot about me. I threw my pack over my shoulders and started back by my lonesome. When I arrive I didn't see a soul. Now I knew I was in trouble.

Hours later H-76 Infantry came back all wet and tired. I was peeking from the window in the barracks.

I hear: "Private Schmidt, report to the Orderly Room immediately!"

As I stood before the first sergeant he wanted to know what happened to me. I told him it started raining and I heard no shooting, I thought they had forgotten me, so I came home.

Well, the top kick kept repeating – "it was raining, and you marched back home."

"Schmidt, for this, you will do two weeks K.P.! And no Indian this time! You heard me, no Indian!"

I did the two weeks.

There were a couple of non-coms in the division who were making life a little unpleasant for me so I got the boxing fever again. I started to train and got into condition and then asked George Thompson, the boxing instructor, to match me with the best man he had in my weight. Nobody knew that I had fought professionally before and I polished off the camp champ with relative ease.

When the fight was over and I was in the dressing room somebody moved a piano and a set of drums into the center of the ring. I hollered for my old pal, Charlie Krider, who played fine piano and specialized in that year's style of boogie woogie, and the two of us put on a rip-roaring show for the men in camp.

I didn't have much trouble after that, I played in the band and ran my little dance orchestra. Five months after I got in the Army they let me out due to demobilization.

11

BEFORE THE WHITE Russian girls started arriving in Shanghai the residents of Shanghai bordellos were mostly American and British women, some French. Many of these girls never left Shanghai. Some died by their own hand or from drink or dope. When they got sick or felt unwanted they usually finished up in one of the "rescue homes" outside of Shanghai.

Many reformed, made good in marriage and went so far as to enter high society in Shanghai, London and New York. A few charming grey-haired matrons are living in Hongkong, Manila and Singapore today, steeped in respectability, frequenting the most exclusive clubs, who had been inmates of a Shanghai "house which was not a home."

No city in the world could hold a half-lit call girl to the refined houses on Kiangsi Road. Visiting Number 52, madamed by the popular Gracie Gale, was like walking into a fashion show. Young women of many nationalities – Russians, British, French, Americans – wore the latest in the world's finest styles, and if you were established all you had to do was to have with you a pencil.

With all her success, however, Gracie Gale had a tragic life. She had a teen-age son in the United States or somewhere. I never knew how much he knew about his mother's business, or where the money came from, but in trying to pull her life together she made the mistake of sending for him to come to Shanghai on a visit.

I DIDN'T MAKE A MILLION

After a time the boy was seen driving around in the best of cars with the most beautiful woman, nightclubbing, drinking, giving it the old wine, women and song routine. The kid was going haywire and it wasn't long before the finger was pointed – like mother, like son. Gracie reluctantly saw her mistake and sailed home with the boy to make arrangements for his college education.

She returned to Shanghai without him. While the ship was docking the Madam of them all took the short route. She committed suicide.

And there was Singapore Kate, one of the most exquisitely beautiful girls I have ever seen. She was also one of the more notorious harlots who traveled up and down the China coast. I heard that as a young girl she lived in Hongkong with an aunt and uncle who grew tired of supporting her when she was about sixteen. They wanted to go to the United States and retire but Kitty, as she was then known, was a problem. They finally induced or forced her to marry a man many years older than she. He professed to love her dearly but she hated him.

It turned out that the man was a sadist. He was very cruel to her. When she could stand it no longer she ran away and boarded a ship for Europe. She was pregnant. By the time she reached Singapore she was too ill to continue, and left the ship. She lost her baby, and after an expensive illness she remained on in Singapore to earn a living and pay her debts the only way she knew how.

Kitty became Kate, and as she broadened her field in the major China outports the name Singapore Kate became a by-word. Her child-like beauty miraculously never seemed to fade. After five years in the Orient she sought greener fields in Europe and boarded a ship for France.

Going up the gangplank she came face to face with the man

she feared and hated – her husband. He was a fellow passenger, whether by design or accident no one knows. He took possession of her, and that night she rushed from her cabin screaming, brutally beaten. A young man in the stateroom opposite came to her rescue and took her to the captain, who put her in his custody for the rest of the trip.

On reaching England the young man took her to his mother's home, obtained a divorce for her and asked her to marry him. She refused, but returned to China with him. After a time she fell ill and the doctors told her it was heart trouble. She was given two months to live. She consented to marry the Englishman, who took her to Dr. Anne Walter Fearn's hospital where she could get rest and care before their marriage.

Dr. Fearn, who was known and trusted by everybody, advised against the marriage. She told the young man it would never work. Singapore Kate was too well-known for them to be happy, even if she recovered.

The young man insisted and they were married in Dr. Fearn's hospital. They had a wedding breakfast at the Astor House and Dr. Fearn introduced her to her friends, trying to be helpful. It was no good. Kate, as she described it, was definitely not knowable.

Strangely enough she recovered from the heart ailment but two years later she died of what was said to be pneumonia. Shanghai knew better. Pneumonia was not the cause. It was a combination of too many men, too much champagne, too much cocaine. She couldn't forget her old profession.

I mentioned that there was a heavy influx of Russian girls into Shanghai which changed the character, or rather the nationality, of popular entertainment. The English, American and French girls, after a few years of steady invasion, were simply outnumbered. Here is how the White Russian invasion got its start.

A salesman by the name of Al Israel from San Francisco arrived

I DIDN'T MAKE A MILLION

in Shanghai in 1919 with a shipload of French champagne. For some reason Al couldn't unload this wine, so he opened the Del Monte Cafe outside the city, on the road that enters the British settlement. The cafe was on the Chinese side. He met the trains coming from Harbin where the White Russians came from, and picked young, beautiful girls who needed work and hired them as hostesses. With beautiful girls and a shipload of champagne, how could he miss?

Al took the girls to the best dress shops and shoe shops and gave them a little advance money. They were stunning. Business got so good that Al Israel went up to Harbin himself and brought back a complete Moscow ballet. The girls would do their show and then act as hostesses.

It wasn't long before Al had to send for another shipload. of champagne, and now girls were arriving at frequent intervals. For the last drink of the evening, usually past daylight, the Del Monte Cafe was a "must" in Shanghai.

In order to give himself more time to find more girls, Mr. Israel brought his brother-in-law, Demon Hyde, out from the States to act as manager and bouncer. It was the same Demon Hyde who "covered" the war with us. Hyde was an exPacific Coast league baseball player but had been working as a "fried spud" (a singing waiter) in some of the joints on the Barbary Coast. (The Demon weighed around 210 – no fat – and for years was one of our mainstays on the Shanghai baseball team saving many a game with his pinch-hitting. He was the Babe Ruth of Shanghai.)

But Al Israel had created a monster. He brought so many beautiful Russian girls in, that he couldn't take care of them all and the other nightclubs began to give them work. These lovelies broke many a marriage. Many of the typans (business executives) married Al Israel's Del Monte girls, but the tie usually didn't last long. As for Al, the guy who started this racket in Shanghai, he finally killed himself.

In the very early part of the White Russian refugee invasion, there came among us a Russian woman of exceptional beauty. I first saw her at the Old Carlton, dancing, with every eye in the house on her and her lucky escort. She was the sultry type, dark-haired, always dressed in gorgeous gowns. They were split up the side to the very limit revealing the perfection of a devastating young figure.

She was the kind of woman who gets talked about, even in sophisticated Shanghai of those days. Her supply of gowns was unending – blue, silver, gold and black. She was a mysterious and intriguing "drifter" as we used to call the refugees.

Eventually we found out who she was, and then she became more intriguing than ever. She was the mistress of the great White Russian general, Ataman Semenov. He had sent her to Shanghai with his jewels and as much of his portable wealth as she could take with her. She glittered with gems. Among other pieces she had an anklet of perfect diamonds.

One night there was a shooting in a place on Broadway involving this beautiful creature. The facts were pretty much hushed up and I knew nothing but rumors for a long time. Finally I got the whole story from Dr. Fearn, who, at one time or another, was called in professionally on the case. This is her story:

It was Semenov's desire that, after a stay in Shanghai, she should continue to Paris where, he thought, she would be safer. She had been committed to the special care of a young Russian officer, tall, handsome and extremely charming. Of course, they fell in love.

During the last days of her sojourn in Shanghai, she begged him unceasingly to accompany her to Paris. Realizing that not only his honor but his life would be the price he must pay for such an indiscretion, he refused. Her steamer sailed at dawn;

the night before her departure, she made her last, impassioned plea in his room. He continued to say no, and to end what was a painful scene for them both, he turned to open the door for her to go and was shot in the back.

She fled to the ship. He was taken to the General Hospital where he steadily asserted that he had shot himself in the back!

The bullet had penetrated the spinal column where it rested on the cord. He was examined by many doctors but, while they all agreed that it was possible to remove the bullet, no one was willing to undertake the operation because of the patient's nationality. Paralysis of the lower extremities set in and in time became complete.

Then Semenov sent a well-known Russian surgeon from Harbin with instructions to operate. But according to the municipal laws governing the General Hospital, a consular certificate was necessary before a permit could be issued to operate there. As no Russian consul was officiating in Shanghai at that time, things reached an impasse. Then Dr. Fearn , being a free lance, offered her private hospital for the operation.

It was brilliantly performed. The Russian worked with the precision of an artist. Dr. Fearn watched him make the incision down the median line, then with chisel and hammer chip away part of a vertebra, and with tiny forceps pick out the bullet which had rested so long upon the spinal cord that it had cut it almost in two. The surgeon held it up.

"The bullet," he said quietly. "Four months too late. He will never walk."

With expert swiftness he freshened the ends of the cord, slightly overlapped and united them and closed the wound. The patient was returned to bed and ordered kept on his face for a week. He bellowed like a bull with pain and discomfort. His groans and cries could be heard for blocks. The disturbance was so terrible that the hospital rapidly emptied and when Dr. Fearn finally reported this state of affairs to the Russian surgeon, he said, "Turn him over, he will die anyway."

As the days passed, however, they ‚noticed that the patient was beginning to move his toes, then his feet, and at last he could lift his legs. It was not very long before he was able to stand, and in time he learned to walk, first with crutches and then with a cane.

At last an order came from Semenov for him to join the lady of their affections in Paris. He left Shanghai with one of Dr. Fearn's Chinese nurse boys who wrote from every port, reporting his progress. Naturally they followed his journey with interest, wondering what sort of future awaited him in Paris. From the different ports they learned of his continued improvement, but the death he had escaped in Shanghai overtook him before he reached Paris and the woman he loved. Several days out from Marseilles he was taken ill with influenza, and on the very day that the ship docked, he died.

Much later Shanghai learned that the lady, on her arrival in France, had been met by representatives of the Reds and relieved of all her wealth. From her position of prominence and riches as Semenov's mistress, she sank rapidly into the obscurity of the Parisian streets.

They came briefly on the scene, these beautiful meteorites of Shanghai night life, and then they disappeared. Sometimes they came back again, not always. But Kiangsi Road, the street of Shanghai's bordellos, seemed to go on forever. Its influence reached out even to the innocent.

One evening I dropped in at the American Club, which was the meeting place for tired businessmen. A friend of mine greeted me, a practicing physician with a solid reputation.

"Whitey," he said, "it's getting so bad that a man can't work

I DIDN'T MAKE A MILLION

at his own profession without suspicion. Read this," and he handed me a piece of paper.

It seems he had been summoned on a sick call to Gracie Gale's place that morning. One of the girls was ill. He parked his car in front of No. 52. While he was inside his wife happened to pass by in her car. She stopped, wrote a note, and stuck it under the windshield wiper of Doc's car where he would not fail to see it. That was the note he handed me:

"DOC, COME HOME. IT'S CHEAPER."

12

THERE WERE OTHER things in Shanghai besides hotels, ballrooms, bars, and houses of ill-repute. For example, we had races on Saturday, Sunday, and holidays, where small Chinese horses were ridden by tall "gentlemen" jockeys. Every racing day was popular, but the grandest affair of all was the "Day of Champions" when all of the best horseflesh and champion jockeys would fight it out on the turf.

On these days you could see the typans strutting around the paddock circles and the club houses, making like big shots and bragging about their horses.

It was customary for the owner of the horse winning the big race of the day to throw the biggest, most exclusive party of the year that night. There were some real lulus. I remember one where a life-sized horse sculptured in ice was wheeled out in the center of a horseshoe-shaped table and champagne and caviar were served out of its hollow body. All the guests received a miniature horse, sculptured from plaster of Paris, to take home.

The English always had the biggest and best stables and there were stake tickets sold on every race. Then, of course, they had parimutuel windows, too. This I know too well. How many times I have walked home shouldn't happen to a horse.

We had golf courses as well, and, of course, remembering my caddying days at the Claremont Country Club in Oakland (one of my odd jobs when times were tough) I took up golf in Shanghai. One day in the Majestic Hotel cocktail lounge I talked myself into a game with three top-flight golfers. Claire Grisswell, who was passing through Shanghai, had just been the runner-up in the Western Open in California. After a few drinks, I talked like an old pro and Mr. Grisswell invited me to play with him and his two friends at the Kiangwan Golf Club.

The next morning, bright and beautiful, who does Claire show up with? The champ of the club, Mr. Joe Ferrier, and Mr. Arthur West, the sports editor of the China Press, who played a mean game, too.

Kiangwan was a finely laid-out course, with Chinese rice paddies on both sides of the fairway. Claire addressed his ball and whacko! straight down the fairway. Ferrier, whacko! on the green. Arthur, whacko! six feet from the pin.

This first hole was 285 yards long, with a 285-yard rice paddy on both sides. The fairway was perhaps a hundred yards wide. I pulled a nice new Silver King out of my bag. That ball sure looked beautiful all teed up there. I stepped back, took a couple of practice swings. Boy, I looked good! As I stepped up to the ball, I was facing the rice paddy, playing for my slice. Whacko! I hit the most perfect ball of the four. But where did it go? Straight into the rice paddy.

Now the three started straightening me out, moving my left foot up, turning my wrist. Whacko! What a shot! What I was looking for the first time, I got this time – a slice. Right over to the other side. Now the Chinese rice planters were looking for my ball on both sides – two out of bounds.

Up I came with my third new Silver King. Whacko! What a beauty! Just good enough to reach the bunker. By this time, the three top-flight men were on the green waiting for me. When I finally rolled mine up with the putter, I was so darn embarrassed that I couldn't sink that damned ball with four putts.

"Score?" I asked as I held the card in my hand. I heard Claire say, "Three," Arthur say, "Three," and Ferrier say, "Three." I said, "Surrender."

No one asked what I made. Claire Grisswell told me, "You know, Whitey, you talk better golf than you play." Now how could this happen? They told me that I had a perfect swing when the ball wasn't there. I was dressed in a better golf outfit than any of them, and my clubs were the best pro set that money could buy.

From that first hole on in, I was spectator and score keeper.

The Americans in Shanghai had a baseball team and it was a pretty good one, too. Each year we looked forward to the Japanese coming over from Tokyo on the fourth of July. We were always looking for baseball talent and took the game pretty seriously.

Our club manager was Herb Gallop and most of our players were good solid business men of Shanghai. But we were not averse to picking up a ball player if he was good, even if he was a hanger-onner or a job seeker just traveling through. If a man could play baseball the typans saw to it that he got a workout.

One fourth of July game with Tokyo the Japanese team was leading three to two in the last of the ninth, Shanghai up to bat. There was one out, one man on base and Jack Riley was in the third base line coaching box. The batter hit a foul down the third base line and Jack Riley retrieved the ball.

Now Jack was always prepared for emergencies. He always carried a pair of dice in his pocket just in case. Likewise, during a baseball game, Jack usually carried an extra ball in his pocket, just in case he might need it in a pinch. It usually was a "rabbit" ball he had in his pocket; especially since the Japanese were leading three to two.

Herb Gallop, the manager, called for time, and had a little talk with Jack Riley. Herb called the great Demon Hyde, the Shanghai Babe Ruth, to pinch-hit and the game was over. Demon hit that rabbit ball so hard over the Shanghai racetrack grandstand that so far as I know they are still looking for it.

I can remember thinking when Demon Hyde hit that ball, about a baseball game in San Francisco in the summer of 1919, before I came to Shanghai. At this particular time I had an old 1913 Model-T Ford. It was underslung to make it look streamlined and then I fitted the chassis with a sports model body. This jalopy was a real whoopty-doo.

There were, however, two things about this car that I didn't like. One was that the back wheel came off when I slowed up; the other was that it was hard to crank in cold weather.

One cold afternoon, after cranking this broncho for half an hour, I got it started and drove it right back in where I got it. I told the garage owner, "Give me seventy-five dollars and you can have this wreck back." Then he got huffy and replied, "If that's the way you feel about it, here." He handed me the seventy-five.

He shouldn't have done that because just two blocks down on Valencia Street in San Francisco was the ball park, and on this particular day there was an exhibition game featuring Babe Ruth's team playing a Lefty O'Doul gathering.

I stopped in to see this game, sitting with the boys at first base. Someone said they would lay a hundred to seventy-five and spot me four runs, taking the Babe's side. Well, I always liked my pal, Lefty, and said that was a bet.

You know, that seventy-five of mine looked like a hundred and seventy-five up until the seventh inning. My buddy, Lefty, had struck out the great Babe three times. It looked good until the eighth. First man walked, the next man bunted. Both men safe. The next man walked and there were three men on with Babe at bat. Whack! Over the fence!

Well, Lefty just kept loading the bags for the Babe, and wack! over the fence. That's the way it was going when I left. I didn't bother about my four-run handicap. All I could hear was "wack", with the shouting in my ears. The fans had their money's worth but Whitey didn't even have his jalopy. He walked.

We had our horse races and baseball games and our golf courses in Shanghai. It was a city where no place of entertainment seemed ever to close. Living was easy but the band and I still worked hard.

One day Mr. Taggert, the managing director of the Majestic, called me into his office. He told me that during my five years in his employ I had accomplished the task I had been given to do. China was dancing, the three million dollar investment was paying off and the future looked good. He said, if I wanted, I could take my wife and go to the States for a vacation. He handed me two envelopes. In one were two first-class roundtrip tickets to San Francisco and four months pay, and in the other a five thousand dollar bonus.

It was 1927, twenty-one years since I had left Denmark. The only cloud on my horizon was the illness of my wife. I knew she was not well and I had my doubts if she would live long.

Florence and I spent four months in the States visitINg our old friends and spending our five thousand dollars. I saw Mama Schmidt and Papa Schmidt and my two brothers. The money I had been sending home to Mama and Papa had been appreciated and they were proud of their son Sven Eric who had run away from home but who had ended up in the bigtime music business in the Orient.

In the back yard at home, that cherry tree my brother had planted over the grave of our little dog, Prince, had grown and flourished until it seemed to cover the whole premises. When in bloom it was one of the sights of the neighborhood and our friends would bring' people to see it.

13

THE TRIP WAS GOOD for Florence and her health seemed better when we returned to Shanghai. The band had been carrying on all the time that we had been gone and Mr. Taggert told me that to keep everybody happy I should take my band for a month's all-expenses-paid vacation to Hong Kong.

We stayed at the beautiful Repulse Bay Hotel, an exquisite Oriental mecca across the island from Hong Kong, and the boys and I really lived it up. When we arrived back in Shanghai, the China Press printed our individual pictures on the front page with a banner headline and the Hong KongShanghai Hotel Company presented me with a new automobile complete with chauffeur. We were back in business.

After our vacation and rest, having seen new people and new things our music seemed to be rejuvenated and the spirit of our organization was at high ebb. We were packing them in every night and our Sunday afternoon tea dances continued to bring the capacity eighteen hundred.

The people who stopped at the Majestic Hotel usually were royalty, celebrities or executives. Douglas Fairbanks, Sr., and his charming wife, Mary Pickford, visited us in 1929. There were thousands and thousands of Chinese waiting outside the hotel to get a glimpse of them. It was just like any American city when a celebrity comes to town.

When Douglas and Mary first arrived I was asked to come to their apartment to arrange the music for Mr. Fairbanks' entrance into the ballroom that evening. He seemed to be in a talking mood so after we finished discussing the music score we had a long chat over a bottle of Scotch and some soda. During our conversation, Mary peeked her head in through the door to remind Douglas that thousands of people were waiting outside to see him. He said, "Just a minute, Mary, I want to tell Whitey just one more thing." And he told me a story that I never shall forget.

He told me of the biggest mistake he had made and the most regrettable thing that he had done in his life. When he was in England a group of charity promoters pleaded with him to endorse certain products for purposes of advertising. They told him that would mean ten thousand pounds – forty thousand dollars – which would go to an orphanage and hospital for children. He readily agreed, not realizing what the effect would be. For after all, Douglas Fairbanks was an athlete and admired by all the youngsters and teenagers for his physical ability and clean living. Douglas told me that for years he had been receiving letters from parents, children, schools and the like berating him for recommending this particular product. It was cigarettes.

When he finished, he got up and said something about that's how life was sometimes and went out to greet his fans. But his sincerity made an impression on me that is as strong today as it was in 1929.

It seemed celebrated visitors from all over the world beat a path to our hotel door. There were people like John McCormack, the Prince of Sweden, Hal Roach, Fritz Kreisler, Jack Pickford, the Duke of Kent, Galli-Curci, the Prince of Denmark and many, many others. Among the many others was a handsome, flashy young man who sent a message one night to the bandstand asking me to join his table. His name was Jess Fry, and he introduced me to two ladies at his table who I knew to be Madams from Kiangsi

I DIDN'T MAKE A MILLION

Road.

Champagne was flowing like spring water and being unable to avoid his insistent hospitality I found it increasingly difficult between dance sets to go back up on the stand to lead the music.

"You know, Whitey, I remember you when you played at Tait 's in San Francisco. It's sure good to see you, but where can we go later to enjoy ourselves?"

I was glad to get rid of him temporarily, so I could wrap my band up for the night and told him to go out to the Del Monte Cafe and I would meet him there later. I arrived there about four a.m., and Mr. Fry was really going good by that time. Demon Hyde rushed over to me when I arrived and asked, "Who in the heck is this guy"? I told him that I didn't know, that I had just met him.

"His bill is up to two thousand dollars now!" exclaimed Demon, "and he has sixteen girls at his table with a bottle of champagne in front of each one."

Just in case Jess couldn't pay, and me not knowing him, I told Demon that the best he could do was to collect his money because I didn't want to be stuck with the bill.

Jess made a great show out of pulling a roll of bills from his pocket. It was fat enough to choke the Mississippi River. He not only paid his tab in full, but he gave the waiter three hundred dollars. Then he asked me how much the band would charge just to go along for another party. I said two hundred dollars and he said, "Don't be a cheapskate! Here's three hundred!"

Jess and Hyde called ten taxicabs and we took all the girls and the band over to Gracie Gale's. Gracie threw the place open to us. The champagne corks began to pop, the band was playing, the girls were screaming and dancing and I was having the time of my life. Everything was on Jess Fry.

At the top of the rumpus Jess undertook to show us the

Adagio dance and the old Indian trick of eating glass. He gnawed and chewed his high-ball tumbler until blood was running down both sides of his mouth and before I could stop him he had swallowed some of the chips.

At this point Gracie was beginning to worry about her bill. It's not every night that somebody buys out the house, and when that somebody starts to eat glass it's time to collect the bill before it is too late. Gracie's hospitality came to three thousand dollars and then I rushed Brother Fry to the hospital.

He survived, and I found out the reason he had so much money was that he had just collected a half million dollars for delivering smuggled arms to the rebels.

One morning later on Jess woke me up from seldom-experienced sleep at five o'clock in the morning. I stood there bleary-eyed thinking if there was one person I didn't want to see at that time of morning, it was Brother Fry. He wanted to know if it was true that I planned to open a new night club of my own and if so, did I need capital? I invited him into my kitchen and over a few cold ones I convinced him that I didn't intend to open anything but the next bottle of beer.

Then he told me that he had $20,000 with him that he had intended to invest in my new night club, but since I wasn't going to open one he suggested that the two of us go upstairs and play the Wheel. (On the top floor of my apartment house on Bubbling Well Road there was a famous Wheel run by a Mr. Garcia, whom I met again, by the way, in Reno, in 1947).

Needless to say, with the combination of Jess's condition and my still being half asleep, it didn't take us long to get breakfast on Mr. Garcia for the twenty thousand dollars we lost.

On another occasion Jess Fry was playing poker with General Morris Cohen. It was a head-on game with a fifty thousand dollars sit-in. I was there watching and once in a while since I

I DIDN'T MAKE A MILLION

was their mutual friend, they would ask me to settle some of their petty disputes. Then they asked me if I would like to play. But I told them that would be ridiculous because I had only four hundred dollars on me and besides that, I had never owned fifty thousand dollars at one time. But they insisted and I sat in with my measley four C's.

Before long I could tell that they weren't trying to squeeze me out and I was still the dispute settler. They were telling me when not to raise and even when to get out. At dawn I counted my winnings and I had six thousand dollars. It was time to go home,

But my friends, said the only way they would stand for my cashing in would be if I promised to stay until they finished. It was the lesser of two evils so I agreed. Then those two started to play poker in earnest. Two days later General Cohen had won Jess Fry's fifty thousand dollars stake.

Both Jess Fry and General Cohen were among the best when it came to cards and when they played it was a sight to see. I was reading an article which mentioned Jess's prowess as a poker player in Chicago, I believe it was. It seems Mr. Fry was in a bar that was the hangout for newspapermen, actors, authors, and the like, when somebody, probably Jess, suggested a poker game. The bartender, anxious to protect his clientele, called Jess aside after play had been going on for a while and Jess had most of the money. The bartender suspected Brother Fry of, shall we say "manipulating" the cards, and told Jess that the gang he was taking to the cleaners actually couldn't afford to lose.

Jess Fry asked for twenty minutes more which the bartender reluctantly gave him, mostly because there was nothing else he could do. Jess went back to the table, stacked the cards against himself and at the end of twenty minutes everyone had his money back.

Jess stayed on in Shanghai for years and I saw him later in

WHITEY SMITH

Manila. Broke or prosperous, he always lived in the best hotels and had the most beautiful women at his beck and call. He always wore a carnation in his buttonhole because if he had just thrown away one of his many fortunes his credit was always good with the flower girl. She knew there was another fortune just around the corner.

14

I've said that musicians, as a lot, were the zaniest, most irresponsible people in their private lives that you could become associated with. If it was true in America it was doubly so in China. I was speaking, of course, of the kind of musician who would go to China and play in a night club band. That lets out the long-hairs and the opera stars (although I've seen a few of those who could qualify) and, seriously, those who make a career of fine music and devote a lifetime to the study of it.

I can think of only one professional group in Shanghai that could give the musicians a run for their money in the zany field. It was the newspaper people, the ones like Percy, for example, who used their newspaper jobs for making connections with gun-runners and the like. They were not numerous. A lot of hard-working, serious-minded newspaper chaps became my friends in the Shanghai days. It was a "good" newspaper town. Four daily papers in English prospered in various degrees, from the staid, solid old British-owned North China Daily News to the struggling little Shanghai Evening News and Mercury, which was run by a dummy board of directors in Tientsin and owned sub-rosa by the old war lord, Marshal Chang Tso-lin. He kept it going because he wanted a newspaper for his own purposes when he conquered Shanghai, which he always expected to do but never did. He was killed in the bombing of a railroad train near Mukden, Manchuria, in 1928. The Evening News later became the Evening Post & Mercury.

WHITEY SMITH

There was J. B. Powell's China Weekly Review, the Japanese-subsidized Far Eastern Review, and a handful of lesser journals. All the big American and British press associations had representatives there, and some of the larger papers in Europe and the United States had resident correspondents.

The more prosperous papers like the Daily News, the China Press and the Shanghai Times had fairly large staffs and frequently picked up "drifters" who came to Shanghai for a year or two then moved on for one reason or another. I remember one young cub named George Leonov who got into the kind of trouble that called for community action. He wrote up an article that slandered some people and was found to be a total untruth. A group of businessmen grabbed him one night, pushed him into an open lot on YuYuen Road and forced him to swallow the full contents of a bottle of castor oil. George left as soon afterward as he was able, for parts unknown.

Among the other newspaper characters in Shanghai in 1929 was Hal P. Mills, who became my best friend of the press. Hal was a mischievous sort and while he often deviated from the truth in his articles he never slandered anybody and was always highly amusing. He carried a cane and sported a Charlie Chaplin mustache, in order to be identified as a correspondent, he said.

One evening, I was standing before my band when a dignified woman danced past and looked up and said, "Mr. Smith, I admire you so much for what you did. It was wonderful of you and so human. How is your foot?"

Needless to say, I didn't know what she meant. I hemmed and hawed, "yes, yes," and started to limp, because right away I suspicioned that Hal Mills had printed something about me in the papers. I hobbled out to the hotel library and shuffled through all the newspapers of the day. Sure enough, I found an article with a head like this: "Majestic Hotel Band Leader Saves

I DIDN'T MAKE A MILLION

Life of Small Dog in Nanking Road."

It went on to say that Mr. Whitey Smith saw this little puppy running down the middle of the street in between traffic. Picking up this little creature, Smith brought it back to safety, but in doing so, his foot was run over by a car. So for a week I had to limp and walk with a cane.

It seemed Hal Mills had a weakness for dogs. He ran another article in the paper and gave it to one of the press associations which put it in print all over the world. I received a newspaper clipping from my hometown Oakland Tribune which had me decorated by the Prevention of Cruelty to Animals Association in Shanghai.

The story was that while I was standing down on the Bund waiting for friends to arrive by boat, a Chinese came along and threw a little puppy dog into the harbor water, shouting, "bad joss, bad joss," which means bad luck. I was supposed to have doffed my coat and jumped into this dirty and treacherous harbor, throwing the dog up on the wharf and saving the poor little mutt's life. For this I was supposed to have been awarded a medal. The punch line is that I can't swim.

Hal Mills, besides being my unofficial press agent, was instrumental one time in getting me a brand new Buick automobile. Here's how it happened:

At the Capital Club one evening in Shanghai I was lamenting the fact that I couldn't rake together twelve thousand Shanghai dollars to buy the new model Buick I had seen that day in a show window. I was watching the crap game and the dice stopped in front of me. "Your dice, Whitey," said the dealer. But I turned them down because I didn't feel like gambling and I had no confidence.

But Mills, who was in the game, laid five dollars down on the line and asked me to shoot for him, I shrugged and threw the cubes out with a couldn't-care-less attitude and Wham! I passed. Three passes later I lost my nonchalance. Hal was drawing down every two or three passes, but I made seventeen in a row. Hal had twelve hundred dollars and gave me half.

From that point on there was no stopping me. I told myself it was either Buick or bust and at four or five in the morning I cashed in my chips. Whitey Smith rode in style in his new Buick the next day.

There was seldom a day that he didn't have the name Whitey Smith on the front page linked with some celebrity. For example, when John McCormack, the Irish tenor, stopped at the Majestic on a tour of the Far East, Hal headlined, "Whitey Smith Entrances John McCormack, the World Famous Irish Tenor, With his Smooth Renditions of Irish Melodies." (This story, of course, appeared after Mr. McCormack's ship had pulled out.)

Always before John McCormack left the dining room for his concerts he put away anywhere from two to four bottles of champagne, "to put a velvet coat on his throat," his manager said. His eating he did after the concert. On his return from the concert hall I would play most of his program for dancing, like Irish Eyes Are Smiling, Mother Macree, My Wild Irish Rose, and so on.

Hal P. later on was a busy man, writing for a syndicate of Chinese papers. He occupied a private office facing the front of Avenue Edward the Seventh in the French concession. In his columns, Mills gave the communists a hard time because of which he received letters of threats and warnings daily, but he kept on giving them hell.

The Commies didn't like this at all, and just for meanness they threw a bomb into his office one day. But Hal, by chance, had chosen that time to see a man about a dog. Instead of lying low to escape trouble he was even more vicious in his attacks. One day he received a tightly wrapped shoe box which contained a Chinese human head. A note read, "Your head is next if you don't leave China now." Hal didn't leave, but he closed his office and did his writing in his room at the Astor House, more defiant than ever.

The Commies never got Hal but the Japanese gave him a bad time. In the years before the Japanese invasion they were just as much a menace to China as the communists – more so really because the Japanese were obviously a foreign power bent on conquest while the communists were Chinese and their connection with Moscow was secret. Hal kept needling the Japanese in his columns and made them furious. When World War II began Hal Mills was arrested and locked up in the Bridge House, the Japanese military prison of horrors. To this day he carries scars of a Japanese bayonet.

This gets me slightly ahead of my story but I want to put in here the adventure of a group of American and British correspondents who ran a battle from the top of a water tank. This was in 1931 and the battle was a by-product of the Manchurian Incident, so-called. The Japanese had thrown in a force to wipe out Chinese resistance in the native settlement across the river, Pootung it was called. In the course of the fighting a Chinese patrol had been cornered by a Japanese contingent which outnumbered them. The Chinese were trapped in a section with a lot of narrow alleyways.

Nearby on the boundary of the foreign settlement was a high water tank on top of which the correspondents had climbed to get a birds-eye view. To keep from being noticed they were lying on their stomachs, taking pictures and making notes, watching the two factions trying to out-figure each other. The Chinese had been getting the worst of it and were nearly snared. Now the Japs surprised them as they came around a dead-end corner. The

Chinese were frozen.

Meanwhile, up on the water tank, seeing the tide of battle going the wrong way, the correspondents tried to balance things a bit by giving hand signals to Chiang's boys. When the Japs moved up, for example, the fourth estate would hand-wave the Chinese back and it wasn't long before the timing was all in favor of the Chinamen. They were knocking off the Nips by the dozen.

The Japs figured this was unnatural and concluded the enemy was getting some hot tips from the outside. They checked every place except up, but the next time they came around that dead-end corner they spotted the signallers and shot hell out of the water tank, wounding a number of correspondents. They got the Chinese, too, but nothing could be done since "he who interferes with trouble, gets trouble."

I tell that story to show that not all foreign correspondents covered their wars from the premises of a large, safe, well-lighted and well-stocked bars, as I must say did happen in a few instances. The word somehow got around that it was established practice, but that wasn't the truth. Those who indulged in this kind of reporting were few in number and of the type which would come to China for two weeks and then write a book about it, talking like an expert.

15

It was those fabulous years of the late twenties that made Shanghai a fascinating by-word in the cosmopolitan set all over the world. It drew adventurers like a magnet. One Sunday afternoon in 1928 I was sitting in the lobby of the Astor House when a distinguished-looking gentleman introduced himself to me as Sir Jackson White from London. We got into conversation and Sir Jackson introduced me to his partner, an American promoter from England named William Conklin. He was equally distinguished-looking but talked even faster than Sir Jackson.

First thing Mr. Conklin wanted to know from me was did I want to make a million dollars. I was a sucker for that line because it was always in the back of my mind that was what I was going to do when I went to China, make a million dollars.

Well, it seemed these two gentlemen were interested in promoting a game called Jai Alai. I had never heard of it up to that time and Sir Jackson undertook to explain it to me. It was a game of Spanish origin played in a large three-sided court. A small hard ball was tossed from wall to wall in basket-like extensions of the player's arm. It was very fast and attracted huge crowds. Under Sir Jackson's deft manipulation of words and gestures the game took on fascinating proportions, especially the description of the gambling and money-making possibilities.

All I would have to do to make my million was to perform an introduction to some wealthy Chinese who would invest his money. I laughed it off at first and bought them a drink but they were persistent. One thing led to another and I found myself daily digging into my pocket for loans and paying their bills. Before I knew it they were into me for eleven hundred Shanghai dollars. I would have to do some fast thinking to get it back.

The idea struck me that we had an International Club in Shanghai operated by five or six local businessmen who had been promoting boxing. The club was heavily in debt. Why not persuade the five owners to turn the organization over to us for promotion, combining Jai Alai with other games? Sir Jackson and Mr. Conklin said what were we waiting for, that was just the thing.

I made the introductions and we had an international sporting club on our hands. It was decided to put up a large auditorium in the French concession. The rights had to be okayed in France, which would take at least three months, during which time I seemed to have a couple of expensive dependents on my hands. To save on overhead I moved a couple of extra beds into my apartment for Sir Jackson and Mr. Conklin. Florence had her own quarters at the Astor House.

They were appreciative but mischievous. One night, on their way to the apartment, they met a punchy, broken-down old negro fighter named Joe Hall. They bawled him out for going around in that shape (he was reeking with cheap booze) and without a place to sleep when his friend Whitey Smith had a bed for him.

So when I get home after work about four a.m. and turned on the lights, what do I see? Something like a dark cloud laid out on my pillow. I bellowed at the cloud and told it to get the hell out of my bed. The cloud said Mr. Conklin and Sir Jackson had told it to sleep there. I straightened out a difference of opinion as to who was boss in that apartment and ordered the occupant out of bed, into his clothes and out of the apartment. I was so sore I took a turn around the block to cool off.

I DIDN'T MAKE A MILLION

On my return coming up the stairs I meet the same dark cloud coming down, wearing my new suit and straw hat. It said Mr. Conklin had dun told him Whitey said he could have the clothes and thanks very much. I burst into the apartment and turned on the lights again. Mr. Conklin and Sir Jackson were peeking through a small opening in the bathroom door, doubled up with laughter. Maybe it was funny but I couldn't laugh.

Well, Jai Alai did open finally and with a bang. I was getting thumped on the back by friends who knew I was in on the promotion. "Whitey, you'll make a million out of this! It's sure fire!"

A million dollars? I had a hard time getting two tickets of the opening night. Mr. Conklin said he didn't think he could spare any as the place was sold out.

The Spanish Jai Alai players cleaned up on their contracts which were in British pounds on sky-high exchange, and so, I suspect, did the promoters. When it came to dividing up the profits they forgot all about Whitey Smith. By threat and cajolery I managed to get back my original investment of eleven hundred with the promise of more, but they sold out and left for Europe early one morning.

Of course these characters who stood out from the crowd weren't all crooks and shysters. The good ship ss. *President Hoover* docked on one of her trips in 1928 en route to San Francisco with a wealthy oil man aboard. His name was Joe Grove and he wasn't on the board of directors or anything like that. He was on his first vacation in ten years as superintendent of an oil field down in Burma, loaded with spending money. On a one-night stopover Joe came out to see the world's finest hotel and ballroom. He was introduced to the crowd and the crowd laughed and applauded heavily.

As the night wore on Joe Grove was having the time of his

life. He was a middle-aged man and since he had been down in the oil fields for so long, he was a little behind the times in fashion. He was wearing an old-style rubber collar, a tight-fitting suit with narrow pants, button shoes, and a derby hat. Naturally he was applauded.

Shanghai had him. He said, "Whitey, I'm going to spend my six months right here," and he went out to the ship's purser and got the fourteen thousand dollars he had brought with him out of the safe, cancelling his passage.

Joe also had brought along with him some elephant feet which had been made into waste baskets, and a cigar box full of star sapphires and alexandrites. So at night, after I finished work, we brought along the cigar box and a couple of elephant feet. This made us very popular with the Russian hostesses and the proprietors.

To start things off, Joe would present the boss with an elephant foot, and as we were dancing and drinking with the girls, he would hand out some stones. Were we popular!

Then came the Shrine convention. The Islam Temple arrived from San Francisco.

Joe and I were both 32nd degree Scottish Rite Masons and we decided that we would cross the hot sands. After it was over, Joe made me a present of a diamond Shrine pin and I presented him with a ring. We were buddies. But the time came when Joe was out of stones and elephant feet and our popularity dimmed.

After five Shanghai months Joe wasn't feeling so well and turned into the hospital which was a smart move, since he was dead broke. When he got well I took care of the hospital bills and settled with his hotel. I put him on a ship with a steamship ticket and enough dough for a drink now and then on the way.

We shook hands and Joe said, "Whitey, after I leave, you perhaps will never hear from me. I never write. But I'll never forget you and I'm sure we will see each other again sometime."

Joe didn't know just how right he was.

It astonishes me now on looking back how persistently active the Communists were all during that lush period in Shanghai and how little attention we paid to a dangerous movement. After Chiang Kai-shek took Shanghai the Kuomintang split with the left-wing group including the communists, and, with the help of a Shanghai "strong man" named Dou Yu-seng, they put down incipient rebellion in the city and chased them out, or most of them. But there were many "incidents" which affected the foreign residents if only as spectators and should have ben a warning of what was to come.

At eight o'clock one night I was standing in front of the Astor House entrance waiting for my car. The Soviet consulate was right across the street, covered with bright lights, with the sickle and hammer placed prominently over its door. It was some kind of Communist anniversary and the Commies had their red flag waving in everybody's face. Meanwhile, the White Russians had been sitting in their Little Russia in the French concession, brewing with hatred and vodka. The more vodka they drank the more they hated, and the more they hated, the more vodka they drank. About the time I was waiting for my car at the Astor House they had reached the boiling point and they came spilling across the garden bridge, men, women, and children, screaming Russian curses and waving clubs. The Reds bolted the consulate door and turned off the lights, but the White Russians climbed all over the consulate, breaking windows and throwing rocks. They tore down the Red flag and finally broke down the door. There were two shots and a man, and a woman came rolling down the steps.

The British police arrived and broke up the riot, sending the White Russians back to Little Russia and throwing a cordon around the Soviet consulate I watched the whole thing. Two days later we had one funeral. It was for the brother of the head clerk at the Majestic Hotel.

There was a lot of terror in Shanghai in those years and it was just a prelude of things to come. I remember when Chiang Kai-shek occupied Shanghai and we had martial law and a ten o'clock curfew. One of my musicians, Arthur Carnaro, lived right across the street from the Chinese area in the foreign settlement. One night, after our session at the Majestic, Arthur was walking down a narrow Chinese street on the way home when he saw three human heads stuck on a picket fence with a roughly painted sign lettered in Chinese characters. It was Arthur's own fence. He turned and made one leaping jump and ran for my apartment, all out of breath. He was trying to tell me what happened and could do nothing but stutter.

I asked him what did the sign say. "I didn't stop to find out. Can I sleep here tonight, Whitey? I'm moving tomorrow."

Human heads on picket fences were not the only things that disrupted a man's normal sleep. At the Astor House, Florence's room faced the back part of the hotel. At night, in the summer time, it was not unusual for us to leave the door half open for ventilation.

One early morning we were sound asleep when someone reached under the net grabbing me by the neck, shouting, "What the hell are you doing in my bed?" He dragged me to the door, gave me a boot in the pajamas and out I went. It was four o'clock. I'm out in the hallway in my pajamas and some stranger is in my room. This was an unhealthy situation so I opened the door and walked back in. The lights were on now and my wife was standing in a corner in her nightgown, screaming.

I was ready to start swinging but this was no small man I knew, since he had lifted me by the neck with one hand. So I let him talk.

"Please forgive me, I've had too much to drink and lost my way. I thought someone was in bed with my wife. I have the room next door."

It turned out he was a lieutenant commander of the United States Navy.

16

WE WERE STILL riding high at the beginning of 1929, my band and I. China was dancing and the younger set had begun to show up in new styles. The Chinese coed was unbuttoning her tight collar and lowering her neckline. She had thrown away her low-heeled satin slippers and started to wear high heels. And she was creating her own innovations with the slit skirt.

At first skirts were slit only on the right side, up to the knee. Before long the left side was slit as well, and the knee was no stopping point. It went thigh-high. And the young Chinese girl in Shanghai in 1929 had the latest American hairdo. Bobs were popular.

I guess we thought our way of life was going on forever. We should have known better. Good fortune doesn't cling to everybody indefinitely when they are living that fast. My first serious blow came in February. Florence died almost without warning. I knew she hadn't been well since her brief recovery on our trip back to the States, but. . . well it kind of cut the ground out from under me. Things weren't the same, but I had to keep on working.

Joe and Nellie Farren came to Shanghai in 1929 and I started them in their dance and song act at the Majestic Hotel. After six months, I asked Joe if he could teach the local Russian girls some routines, since our imported shows never lasted long. As the foreign girls would hit the pace of Shanghai night life, many would either fall in love, hit the bottle, or get homesick and leave.

I DIDN'T MAKE A MILLION

Many ended up on Kiangsi Road.

Joe Farren selected twelve girls out of hundreds who turned up for audition and after three months of drilling and costuming, Joe and Nellie opened at the Majestic Hotel with their "International Review." Everybody wanted to know where the girls came from.

They lasted together for years and played in other parts of China after Shanghai.

Then Joe opened his Farren's Club outside of town. He had a gambling casino which was backed by the famous Jack Riley. Jack played ball on the Shanghai baseball team, the chap I referred to earlier as providing the "rabbit ball" for that Fourth of July game with the Japanese team. He was the type of fellow who didn't drink or smoke and had only to worry about the other vices.

Jack Riley, in time, became one of the most famous characters who ever arrived in the city. With his first crap winnings he smuggled in a couple of slot machines in parts. The first consignment brought to him was listed as picture frames. The next was supposed to be the machinery for clocks. Then, hokus pokus, slot machines!

It wasn't long afterwards that Jack was the slot machine king of Shanghai and was seen daily driving down Nanking Road in that year's best car with a couple of blondes in the back seat.

One night Jack was out on a coffee binge dancing with his favorite girl at the Canadrome ballroom where they featured a fourteen piece negro band from Chicago. The leader of this organization was a trumpet player who stood in front of his band. As Riley danced, he imagined that this horn tooter was flirting with his girl, so the next time around, Jack let go a Sunday punch, hitting the colored boy right on the chin. He ended up under the grand piano.

The ballroom was in a commotion. Jack was ducking

saxophones, guitars, trombones, and fourteen colored boys were on his neck. The last seen of the "king" that night was when he ran out the front door with a trombone bent around his head.

I remember an exclusive dinner party about that time given for Generalissimo Chiang Kai-shek in the Gold Empire Room. I was asked to give my interpretation of what Tin Pan Alley was. I must have given him an entirely different idea than he had originally if he had any at all because he laughed immoderately and talked with explanatory gestures to the people he was with.

The Fox Newsreel director, Mr. Bonny Powell, shot movies showing the Chinese dancing to the latest American music. In this picture I featured a song written by two members of my band, entitled, "When It's Night Time In Dear Old Shanghai And I Am Dancing, Sweetheart, With You." It sounds kind of corny now but I made a Victor record of it and we sold thousands to the Chinese. It was so successful, as a matter of fact, that it later became part of the Magic Carpet series.

My band made a record now and then for local companies too. Once in a while, I would even write a little tune and if it went over, I made a recording of it. I wrote one I called A Chinese Wedding, but I was stuck for a real Chinesey introduction. While in a department store one day I heard a Chinese girl singing accompanied by a Chinese fiddler. I asked the clerk what the song meant and he replied, "Man, wife, plenty trouble. Wallow! Wallow! Wallow!" That sounded like my answer so I asked the singer and accompanist to come to the studio to record.

After a thousand records had been released to the public I found through a friend of mine that the introduction I had worked so hard to get was really an old Jewish chant that the singer had picked up. So right away I had to recall my records, and palmed them off on the president of a local company who had just returned from the States. Within a month's time a sign in one of his record shop windows announced, "Buy one of our records and receive one of Whitey Smith's Free."

Up to now I was still in clover. The stock market was crashing in the States, but I still had my band earning a good salary and only the death of my wife to cast a pall over my life. My heart wasn't in my work.

Then without warning the Majestic Hotel was scheduled for sale. I had two months' notice, six months' pay, and first class transportation back to the United States. And to make it easy on us they gave us six months to use or forfeit our passage.

With things on the downgrade in the States, I didn't think that it would be a smart move to take my band there. Although we were well-known in the Orient and as good as most of what they had back home, jobs would be scarce and competition pretty tough. So I got in touch with Paramount Picture Corporation in Tokyo and after some negotiation they offered me a contract to play a Japanese chain of theaters. I talked it over with the band and they all agreed to go. But I was in for a shock. At lunch one day the headwaiter, Mr. John Rieger, made some kind of remark about where was I going to get a new band to take to Tokyo since most of my boys had contracted with the new owners of the Majestic Hotel to stay right where they were.

It was hard for me to believe what I heard. I had always had faith in my men and they never double-crossed me. I just couldn't accept the fact that they would go behind my back after seven years. But I had to find out the truth so that night I screened every member and all I got was a few indefinite yes's and no's. Then I knew that the German waiter was right and I went home and cried. I felt like a real outcast.

Next morning my guitar player, Russell Ellis, gave me a call. He was one of my loyal members and told me that the new owners of the hotel, the Sun Insurance Company, wanted to see me immediately. So I hurried down to the office and talked to a Mr. Lee Tan who wanted to know why I was not interested in staying at the Majestic ballroom. Now I knew there was something rotten in Denmark.

I informed Mr. Tan that I had been told the insurance company would not meet my price. There was a surprised look on his face and he asked me what my price was. He was even more surprised when I told him that it was the same as I had been getting. So we signed a contract for six months. It's a good thing we did. I was so deep in debt that I couldn't have left Shanghai and this contract saved the day for me.

That night I told the band to get out arrangement number sixty-five. The title of this song was "Victory" which was printed in big black letters across the top of the arrangement.

"The next time you pull a double-cross," I told them, "don't tell the waiters about it. Go to the top and talk to the boss. I have the contract. I'm staying, and as of now, with a few exceptions, you all are leaving."

It was difficult for me to break up my wonderful organization but it was something that could not be avoided. I still had my contract and I scrounged the city for suitable musicians to make up a new band. I had American, Filipino, Russian, and German musicians and I called my new outfit "Whitey Smith's International Band", and during the next six months I made more money than I did with my all-American outfit. I'll admit it wasn't the same. The music wasn't as good and it wasn't as much fun. But the crowds were almost as big and I carried out my contract and paid off my debts.

17

It was time for me to head back for the United States and I knew it. I took my eight hundred dollars' savings – which when you come right down to it wasn't a heck of a lot of money after all I had been making – and undertook preparations to go home. Whenever I change course or make a new move something happens or somebody turns up to either make things worse than they are or to help me. As usual, it happened this time, and it was not helpful.

The night before I sailed, upon leaving a big party that friends had set up for me, I ran into a short friendly fellow who asked me if I was Whitey Smith. Since I was, I told him yes. Right away he began giving me his sad story. He said he was "on the beach" and would I help him get back to the States. If I would buy him a third class ticket on the ship I was taking he would return the money to me on our arrival in San Francisco. His sister, he promised, would put up the dough.

He looked so darn sad I told him to meet me next morning in the lobby of the Cathay Hotel. He said his name was Jack King and he had been working as an entertainer in Marie Meredith's Little Club. Well, I gave him a couple hundred bucks and we boarded the ship together. Jack stood shoulder to shoulder with me at the rail, waving good bye as the ship pulled away from the dock.

Aboard the same vessel was one of the most charming girls I had ever known. She was a ballet dancer and temperamental as a race horse. Her name was Miss Panova. Before we had left the Woosung River and entered the East China Sea I renewed our acquaintance and confided to her that I was afraid my new-found friend Jack was a moocher. He was already into me for two hundred and I still felt sorry for him on account of the sad story he told me. I said I thought I needed someone to protect me from my own soft-headed generosity and more as a joke than anything else I stuffed my remaining roll into a big handbag she was carrying.

That evening we were sitting in deck chairs enjoying the sea when Mr. Jack King showed up. He was pleasant enough and we chatted about show business and Shanghai. Suddenly Muska's little Pekinese dog bounded out of her lap and down the deck, and of course we bounded after him. Jack stayed where he was.

We recovered the dog and returned to enjoy the evening some more. Jack drifted off. Muska still had my money and she opened her handbag – which looked the size of a steamer trunk – to count it and give it back to me. Lo and behold, it was two hundred dollars short! Muska was mortified and bewildered and started to cry.

I suspected Brother King and told Muska so. Then she said that she remembered opening her bag while we were on the deck and she saw the reflection of Jack King's face in her mirror as he looked into it. It was simple enough to deduct what had happened. While Muska and I chased the mutt, Jack dipped into the purse and helped himself to another two hundred skins.

The next morning we dropped anchor at Kobe and Jack came to me and said that the immigration people would not let him ashore unless he could show some money. I thought back about the four hundred dollars I would still have if I had never met this louse, and gave him a cuff on the chin. Outside of the satisfaction I got, this move did me no good. He didn't have a cent on him.

I DIDN'T MAKE A MILLION

I thought the thing over and left the ship with my mind made up. I found Jack in the writing room of the Kobe Hotel. The nogoodnick was sending money – my money – to himself in San Francisco. But I couldn't prove it.

Back aboard ship I was real friendly – with one hand on my wallet – and bought him all the drinks that he could take. He was very talkative and I found out what hotel he planned to make his headquarters when we arrived Stateside. I was so interested in playing detective that I missed half the pleasures of the voyage.

In San Francisco I went to the Embassy Hotel and buttered up the clerk and he told me (a) Mr. Jack King was stopping there, (b) he had received mail on arrival, and (c) he had paid his rent in advance with a hundred dollar bill. My case was complete.

I called Jack on the telephone and asked him to come down to the lobby. He had a guilty conscience because the first thing he said to me when he approached me was, "You still think I stole that money from you, don't you?"

It sounded kind of corny, but I replied to him "Jack I know you stole it, but I'm not going to do anything about it now because it's rats like you who end up in jail! And I'll see you there. I'll have nothing to do with putting you there, remember that, but I'll see you in jail."

And with that dramatic line I walked out to find what the word "depression" meant. I wasn't finished with Jack, however.

The first thing I did was to go home to Mama and Papa Schmidt. Things were different this time but I tried not to let my parents know about it. I was no longer on top of the world. I had made my splash in Shanghai. I didn't have a band any more and instead of a five thousand dollar bonus in my pocket I had less than three hundred dollars. I didn't know where I was going and I was once again just plain Sven Eric Heinrich Schmidt, a few years older and only a few bucks richer than when I sneaked over the back fence with my set of drums that Papa Schmidt bought with his last sixty-five simoleons.

If I had come home as a refugee from a lamasery in Tibet Mama Schmidt would have given me the same affectionate loving understanding welcome that I would have received had I just been elected to the presidency of the United States of America. Only I didn't fool her one darn bit.

I grubbed around for a few months trying here and there to land a spot of work. I wasn't having much luck until I ran into an old friend, Walter Beban, who at one time played solo saxophone with the famous Art Hickem band at the St. Francis Hotel. He told me that he was with the National Broadcasting Corporation producing radio shows and his big success at that moment was the Spotlight Review.

Walter said that he could make arrangements for me to have an audition if I had a band.

I didn't exactly have a band but I knew of one which had rehearsed for three months for a hotel job which fell through. The aggregation was set up with the best musical talent in the city, but it seemed that the leader didn't have the selling touch, and gave up. I took over this sixteen-man organization and was the first band to have an audition in the new San Francisco NB studio.

After the audition was over I was told that the NBC officials rated our band on equal terms with the Lauffner and Phil Harris band at the St. Francis and that I should stand by since there was a contract in the making in Spokane, Washington, at the Davenport Hotel. There was a radio station on top of the Hotel and NBC was trying to get them merged.

While I was waiting, NBC had us play a few one-night stands, but this was during the depression and it wasn't enough to keep the men in grub. Some of the boys took other jobs out of town and then I was offered a job to play at Calneva Lodge, near Lake Tahoe. I selected eight men and grabbed it. After three weeks Walter wired me to be ready with the band to leave for Spokane. But I couldn't take the job since I had agreed to stay the season at Calneva.

Bones Remmer and Bill Graham, who ran Calneva, were pretty high up on the gambling totem pole, and in their circle also highly respected. They were pleasant and always treated their employees on the up-and-up. The Calneva Lodge was an attractive club and many Hollywood celebrities frequented the place.

Jack Dempsey was a perennial visitor. We had a lot of fun with Jack but you had always to be on the lookout, because if you weren't, you would end up with one of the famous Manassa Mauler hotfoots and, believe me, having been on the receiving end, I can tell you they were painful.

Jack would sneak up on an unsuspecting victim and crawl under his table, apply the matches, light them and sneak away. By the time they had burned down to the match heads which were jammed between the sole and the uppers, Jack was on the other side of the room watching. The victim usually would go straight up in the air, but no one I knew of ever tried to take physical issue with Jack Dempsey on this subject of hotfoots.

I was worried and down in the dumps. I owed the house money because of my losses on the gambling tables. I was ducking both the cashier and the boss. I hung out most of the time in my room which was downstairs in the club and the scrapbooks with their clippings and pictures from Shanghai didn't help my morale a bit. Believe it or not, I was homesick for China.

One night an attractive middle-aged woman accompanied by a young gentleman came to the club and asked me to sit at their table. I obliged because it meant company, and besides the boss would be reluctant to talk to me about my gambling account while I was sitting at a customer's table.

The young man introduced me to the lady. "Just call me Auntie," she said. His name was Arthur and he spent Auntie's money as though it were potato chips. She had plenty of it apparently. After the club closed we drove down to Reno in her great big Cadillac limousine, complete with colored chauffeur, and did the town. Auntie was living it up in Reno until her divorce became final.

She was a grand woman, but unhappy. The two of them came back every evening. Finally I got around to telling them my troubles and all about my years in Shanghai. Especially Arthur was impressed and one evening when I took them to my little three-by-four room they practically devoured my scrapbook. Arthur made no bones about wanting to go to Shanghai, and at the moment I would have given my left eye to be back there myself.

I had another persistent notion in the back of my head. I had always wanted to try my luck in the Big Town, New York City. And if the truth be told I was more than a little interested in Muska. She was doing all right for herself. Right away after landing in San Francisco she had made contact with New York through an agency on the coast and was booked in the Roxy theater there. I thought if I showed up she might consent to go back to China with me as Mrs. Whitey Smith.

I told Auntie and Arthur about my dilemma and confided to them that more than wanting a career in New York I wanted to go back to Shanghai and open a club of my own. I looked at Arthur and could tell he wanted in on a deal like that, wanted it so badly it showed like a halo. Auntie looked at Arthur and saw the same thing. What a woman. She said she always had wanted to invest in a Shanghai night club. She dived into her well-filled

I DIDN'T MAKE A MILLION

purse and pulled out a thousand dollars.

"Here, Whitey, you take this for a starter and go to New York and see your girl. Afterward we'll see what we can do about setting you two up in business."

18

WHEN I RECOVERED from the shock of this piece of generosity and made sure Auntie and Arthur both understood the thousand dollars was an investment and not a gift, I had to confront another set of facts. I had a contract with Bones Remmer and Bill Graham at Calneva Lodge and they weren't the type of people you broke contracts with. Arthur talked me into at least asking. Bones and Bill told me not only no but hell no.

There was a handyman around the Calneva that had become a pretty good friend of mine. I told him I was going to leave, but that I didn't want Bones or Bill to know about it. He gave me a wink. I had told him a little about my situation. Friend that he was, he took my drums and other belongings and stored them for me. At the propitious time we loaded them into Auntie's car and drove quietly away.

I had figured my finances pretty carefully and came to the conclusion that after paying off my three hundred eighty dollar gambling debt to the club (which I did with part of Auntie's thousand dollars) the six hundred twenty dollar remainder would little more than take care of a ticket by air and expenses. The train was cheap but the bus was cheaper and almost as fast, so the bus it was. We arrived at the bus terminal in Reno, and I said so long to Auntie and Arthur and hopped a Greyhound.

Somewhere along the line Fred Waring's band got aboard (Fred himself was not there) and the trip turned from a dirty uncomfortable bore into a real ball. There was playing and

I DIDN'T MAKE A MILLION

singing and the trip from that time on passed quickly.

Muska had done well for herself. She had met Lita Roberti, who many will remember as the star of the Broadway hit, "You Said It", and others. Lita had taken a liking to her and lent Muska her mink coat and jewelry and introduced her to the big wheel at the Roxy. The Roxy in those days was no small potatoes and Muska had it made as ballerina, besides having a wonderful time. To make a long story short she did not want to go back to Shanghai as Mrs. Whitey Smith.

A week after I arrived in New York I received a telegram which said, "Friends will pick you up and take you back to California." I couldn't quite figure that out, but I thought that Auntie and Arthur knew people in New York and had asked them to pick me up as a passenger on their way west. It didn't make much sense, but I didn't question it. I was darned near broke trying to keep up with the New York crowd and I just stood back waiting for somebody to do something.

Ten days after I arrived I received a phone call. It was Arthur. He and Auntie had driven day and night, from Reno to New York to pick me up. I was fed up and mighty glad to see them. After they had rested a night we started to drive, and except for meal stops again we went straight through to Reno because Auntie had to be in court on a certain day to get her final decree. If she wasn't there she would have to start all over again.

By this time, of course, Arthur had more than ever made up his mind that he wanted to go to Shanghai. And, more than that, he had really convinced Auntie that this was a good thing. As far as Auntie was concerned nothing was too good for Arthur.

She asked me if six thousand dollars would be enough to start a nightclub in Shanghai. I said that I thought I could manage on six grand.

Bones and Bill had not been too pleased with my sudden

disappearance from Calneva but there wasn't the violent reaction I had anticipated. They raised the dickens with me when I returned but I went back to work. Things rocked along for a while. Business was good. People gambled and danced to my music and Auntie and Arthur continued to visit me every night. Shanghai was on all our minds.

Finally I got up enough courage to ask Bones and Bill for a release. They had said no when I went to New York, but this time they agreed – if I could get someone to take my place.

I jumped at this and using my contacts I dug up a man in San Francisco who was satisfactory. Whoopee!

Auntie took Arthur and me to Reno. She stopped at a bank and the first thing I knew I had a letter of credit for six thousand dollars. She advanced some cash on the side for pocket money, too.

On the way to the station I saw a little runt sweeping the street. He was a bit dressed up for doing that kind of work and I looked at him closer. It was that little moocher Jack King. The guy who had stolen my two hundred bucks out of Muska's handbag.

I asked the driver to stop and when Mr. King saw me he said, "Jesus, Whitey! Am I glad to see you!"

"What happened?" I asked.

"I'm doing six months," he answered. "I was in a hotel room and accidentally knocked a coke bottle off the window sill and it hit a guy on the head down on the street."

"Is that so?"

"Yeah. Listen, Whitey, you know all the big shots here in Reno, maybe you can spring me. I'm a trusty so it should be easy."

"Sure, Jack," I said, "I might try to fix it for you, but I told you I would see you in jail and this is the payoff. I'm leaving for Shanghai. So long."

Maybe I had grown up a little. Maybe.

I DIDN'T MAKE A MILLION

Arthur and I took a train to Canada and at Vancouver we boarded the ss. *Empress of Russia*. Just before we left, Auntie presented each of us, since it was prohibition time, with two bottles of an old Crow to keep our spirits up.

The voyage was uneventful and all I could think of was the new club we were going to open. I had wired ahead to my friends that I was coming back to Shanghai but I didn't expect them to meet me at the mouth of the Whangpoo River with a launch carrying a one hundred piece brass band playing, For He's A Jolly Good Fellow! There was a banner around the launch screaming, "Welcome Back To Shanghai, Whitey Smith" and everybody was shooting off fireworks. All my welcomers were wearing straw sombreros, drinking beer from barrels and shouting and clapping their hands. The local cabaret musicians had gotten together with the Fourth Marine band stationed there and they really made a lot of racket.

The launch traveled side by side with the Empress up the twelve miles of river before docking and then the party started. The newspapers said, "Whitey Smith Gets Presidential Welcome," and it was some little time before I got my bearings.

We took the six thousand good United States dollars Auntie had invested in us and converted it into Shanghai dollars. With the exchange at five Chinese dollars to one American, we had about thirty thousand. It was enough to start in business.

We had planned pretty thoroughly. I had the contacts and I knew about where we wanted to locate. We picked a good spot in the Hall and Holtz Building just off Nanking Road on Szechuan, and one auspicious night we opened the Cinderella Club. We had a big sign that looked good at night and of course it had Whitey's name on it. I was in business for myself! – and partners of course.

Arthur was entranced with the novelty of the whole business, just as crazy about Shanghai as I was when I first arrived. I had a lot of experience working in clubs and all the confidence in the world. Arthur didn't know much about the night club business but he was eager and we got along well together. From the first night on we were packed.

We introduced dancing during the two-hour vesper drinking period and furnished good entertainment all night long. The walls of the Cinderella were bulging and my back was sore from the slapping it was getting. Everyone said, "Whitey, you're going to make a million!"

All we had forgotten to figure on and plan for was a war.

19

My troubles and China's troubles seemed to run parallel starting along toward the end of the year 1931, with the Japanese always making the trouble. In September came what the newspapers called the, "Manchurian Incident." It was some incident.

The Japanese always claimed it was started by an attack on their South Manchurian Railway by soldiers wearing the uniform of the Chinese government. That was their excuse for occupying about three hundred and sixty-five thousand square miles of Chinese domain. My friend J. B. Powell always claimed that was the real beginning of World War Two. However that may be, it eventually ruined the Cinderella Club.

We were going great guns. Many visiting celebrities dropped in for a look-see. I will never forget the night when one of our great Americans stepped up to me and said, "My name is Will Rogers. I like your little place here. It makes me forget that I'm homesick."

Mr. Rogers had a beer with me (something he didn't indulge in very often) and while we talked a crowd of Chinese coeds spotted Will and came over with pencils and menus asking for autographs.

He said, pointing to one of the girls, "Whitey, this one looks like a Sioux." Her hair was cut short in a bob style and she did look like an Indian. She wanted to know, "What is a soo?" Will told her and I agreed that she could have doubled for a Sioux maiden any day. Somebody suggested that since the American red man came from the Orient to begin with, maybe they had just left this little gal behind.

There was one outstanding pan-handler hanging around the place who always had the saddest story to tell. This fellow was known as Mickey O'Brien. He had sort of a bent nose and looked like he forgot to duck sometime. Later in years, Mickey went legit and became a bouncer in a joint on "Blood Alley," the toughest street in Shanghai. When World War II broke out he stowed away for Hong Kong; but it wasn't long before the British police picked him up. Mickey said he was an American citizen but he had no papers. Washington never heard of him and there were no records. So the British had Mickey O'Brien on their hands. A man without a country.

Mickey couldn't leave this British colony so he was slated to go back into the clink. He boarded the Macao (a Portuguese colony) ferry and tried to go ashore there. But no, they didn't want him either. So he stayed aboard, making this trip daily for years. Mickey got to be one of the big tourist attractions on both ends. He would receive food and money from sympathizers. It got to be a good business. After the Second World War he became a celebrity. Mickey later on got the ear of the President of Brazil and was allowed to board a freighter for Rio de Janeiro.

Count Ciano, who was married to the daughter of Mussolini, was acting as the Italian consul in Shanghai in 1931. He was a regular party-thrower and having heard my band over the radio he decided to ask me to play at his next party, and when the Cianos threw a party it was a real wing ding.

After we played once we were regular fare. The count would find out first what night I was able to play outside of my club and when he was in the party- throwing mood he would schedule his party accordingly. The guests were usually Shanghai officials, military brass and the Shanghai "four hundred."

One evening the Count was worried about how Il Duce was doing back among the macaroni and cheese and he took me out to one of the big rooms and showed me the silverware. Each piece, I noticed, had the king's crest engraved on it. Count Ciano said to me, "Whitey, could we open a night club on what you see here? Just in case we should have a revolution in Italy, I mean?"

Certainly we could have. But when the revolution finally showed up, I was a prisoner of the Japanese.

Just after the opening of the Cinderella I tried to persuade the British Radio Station to let me broadcast over the station which was known as "XCBL". They were too busy to listen to me so I set out to promote my own station. Before long I found a man who was interested, a Mr. Sid Baumont. He rounded up a one lung transmitter but we couldn't find a place to install it. I moved out the bathtub and other facilities from my own bathroom and that became the Cinderella's radio station. It at least had the distinction of being on the Cinderella mezzanine floor. The only program that went over the air from this bathroom station was my band from twelve to two in the afternoon and from eight to ten at night.

We had two telephones installed on the bandstand and we played all requests possible. It was a matter of but a few days when our time was all taken by sponsors.

Mr. Roy De Lay, the owner of the Electric Service Corporation, had on hand at this particular time about two thousand old style Majestic radios which had been resting on his shelves for months and months. Our Cinderella broadcast became so popular with the Chinese and foreigner alike that he sold all two thousand. By this time the sponsors on station XCBL were screaming that nobody was listening to their programs and threatened to cancel their contracts because of our bathroom station. The board of directors of the British station knew when they were whipped and decided to pay me to close.

Commander Percy Marshall, the managing director of XCBL, asked me how much I wanted to close down the bathroom and move our music and show over to their line. Without batting an eye I said twelve thousand Shanghai dollars and forty percent of all my sponsored programs. It hurt him and he called me a thief of the lowest order, but I got it. Sid, who started with me, got six thousand dollars for his short efforts and I received the best car I could buy with my share as down payment and the balance to be paid by my forty percent. So, I had fun until the Manchurian Incident and curfew went into effect, then the car went into hock.

There was a young fellow coming in to see me at my Cinderella Club nearly every night. His name was Bob Short and he came to China to teach the Army students how to fly. One day at the bar, Bob and I had a drink together and as he left we shook hands and said, "Maybe I'll see you tonight."

But I never saw my friend again. When he got to the airfield a Japanese fighter was overhead and Bob tried to clobber him with an armed training plane which was no match for the Japan combat bird. The whole city of Shanghai watched the battle, which was nip and tuck for a while. But all of a sudden out of the clouds came Bob's plane with smoke trailing from the tail. Bob didn't have a chance with that old dilapidated plane and he knew it when he took off. But that old fighting spirit was there and it was buried with Bob Short in a Nationalist Chinese cemetery, marked with a stone inscribed:

Bob Short, an American
Died a Hero for the Chinese People
1931

Bob's mother made a visit to his grave in Shanghai in 1934 at the expense of the Nationalist Government.

The Manchurian Incident reached down into Shanghai in

pretty short order. The Chinese were so mad at the Japs they started boycotting them and roughing up their citizens, of whom there were many in our city. So Tokyo ordered in troops to occupy Japanese populated areas around Shanghai. By the end of 1931 there was shooting in nearby Chapei and by February of 1932 martial law was declared. The United States Government ordered in the 31st Infantry from Manila to help protect the foreign Settlement, and business just about had to shut up shop all over the city. Everything was very tense. Curfew set in at nine o'clock and lasted until dawn.

The Chinese and Japanese were fighting across the border of the Foreign Settlement, now and then stepping over the line. After nine in the evening, Shanghai was closed tighter than a drum. Anyone on the streets after this hour was picked up for internment until five in the morning. Our band and show had been standing by waiting for some thing to break, so on Saturday nights I opened until nine, and anyone who was there after nine had to stay all night or else go to the klink.

The night club crowd on Saturdays ran from all directions for the Cinderella to make the curfew deadline and once I had them locked in for the night I was the master. After two in the morning the Cinderella looked more like a bunk house than a night club. The customers slept there, heads on tables, on top of the bar, stretched out on chairs, both patrons and employees. They couldn't keep awake. The Cinderella could handle three hundred or so (with four hundred the walls were bulging). There was no air conditioning. Windows and doors were closed – smoke, booze, perspiration. As I walked through the tired crowd I would call the time, dangling my keys. The prisoners of night life would respond in chorus "I want to go home!" When the gates opened in the morning the flock looked to me like sheep running for the green pastures.

WHITEY SMITH

So while the sons of the Rising Sun and Chiang Kai-shek's boys played soldier, there was Whitey Smith with an up-tothen successful club just beginning to pay off its debt, with closed doors. Except for those Saturday nights they stayed closed for four months, with the band and a floor show always hanging around for a cash advance. When the curfew lifted I was right back where I started, thousands and thousands of dollars in debt.

20

WHEN THE CURFEW finally lifted in about four months business was pretty well shot. It was hot season in Shanghai, meaning the weather. Trying to operate the Cinderella under that load of debt was pretty risky I figured and I was looking for a way to get out clean. I contacted a Chinese caterer in town and we came to an agreement. He took over our financial obligations and Arthur and I walked out. He handed me one Shanghai dollar to make it legal.

Arthur had found himself a job in Chefoo, one of the northern outposts where the U.S. Navy hung out and where the night life was even more uninhibited in its way than Shanghai. We parted good friends and no visible regrets. If we had any, we buried them under a grin. Arthur stuck it out until sometime in 1934, then took a boat home.

l hadn't walked a hundred feet from the Cinderella when I saw a sign which said Plaza Hotel. It was a well-known hotel in the French Concession. I had an idea. I went inside and asked for the owner, a Chinese banker named Mr. Low. We had a two-hour chat and ended up being partners in a night club called the Rose Room. He agreed to remodel the ballroom downstairs in the hotel and to put up the cash and I would furnish the music and the shows. So in a matter of a couple of hours I was back in business again for another try at that million.

Everybody said I would sure make it this time because the club was a three-month wonder. But there was a catch. When settlement time came around, Mr. Low would give me only money enough to settle with the band and the show and gave me credit for the balance. There was a run on his bank. Something was missing. I think it was money. So after an argument, I moved out bag and baggage and left Mr. Low with his new remodeling job and the prospect of running it with no band or entertainment.

I stored my instruments in the club across the street and then scouted around to make another deal. I had just "lost" my second million within a matter of a year and a half and I felt that my goose was cooked for at least the time being. I knew I was done when one of my American newspaperman friends whom I had kept in food and drink for years, came out in his newspaper with an article headed, "What Has Happened To Whitey Smith? Does he carry a Jinx?"

That was it! The Chinese are very superstitious, and since all the agents controlling the entertainment world in Shanghai were Chinese, if you will pardon the expression, I didn't have a Chinaman's chance. So I looked toward Japan.

My old friend Demon Hyde knew Bob McIntyre, head of Paramount Pictures in the Orient, with headquarters in Japan. Bob responded to my inquiry with an offer for me and my band to play for one week at the Imperial Theater in Tokyo, and four weeks at the largest theater in Osaka. We were to appear on the stage with one hundred fifty Beautiful Japanese Girls. Ah, so!

We arrived in Kobe in early 1933 and a Japanese band welcomed us at the pier. Somebody had stretched a banner across the landing which read, "Welcome to Japan, Witty Smith." They had my name spelled wrong, but they meant well.

We had one week before opening. There were twelve men in my band which I put up in one hotel and one girl dancer which I put up in another. When it was time to move on to Tokyo for our first week's booking you would have thought my hotel bill was the U. S. national debt. Those twelve musicians found the bar before they found their rooms and I doubt if some of them ever found their rooms at all.

When I got to Tokyo I told the hotel manager that I would be responsible only for the food bill and positively not the liquor bill. I had forgotten the ingenuity of thirsty musicians and let my mind be at ease during the week we were appearing at the Imperial. Before leaving for Osaka the hotel manager presented me with something that looked like a restaurant menu. All that was on there was breakfast, breakfast, a few lunches, a few dinners, and lots more breakfasts. It didn't take long to figure out that every time they had a drink they would sign for a breakfast.

Now the whole band was in debt to me, but nobody had anything coming anyway.

The theater we were booked into at Osaka was enormous, accommodating six thousand people. On stage, during the show, as I said before, there were just twelve men and one hundred and fifty cute little eighteen-year old Japanese girls. From the first night on I was handling twelve wolves. I could have done a better job if I had a fifteen-foot blacksnake whip. All my musicians were hounds for the women and these one hundred and fifty cuties really upset their metabolism. One of the boys was caught in the wings necking one of the chorus girls, and it was reported to the manager. As a result there was a meeting that night after the show when the director stood on his soap box delivering what I guess to be a real stirring speech. He was screaming at the top of his voice and my interpreter told me that the director was telling how the chorus girl had disgraced herself and the rest of the females by being seen kissing one of Witty Smith's Americanos behind the scenes. This apparently really shook the place up because Witty Smith, his band and his lone dancer were fired.

WHITEY SMITH

I was uneasy when I returned to the hotel because since I had not completed our engagement there was no money. When the manager handed me the bill he bowed and scraped and hissed. I looked at the charges and wished that I had never learned to count because the bill was much larger than I could pay. I noticed that all the boys' chits came from the Japanese fish grotto there in the hotel and what did I see? Raw fish, cold lobster, cracked crab, octopus eyes. There were many, many orders of raw fish and I knew that I had been had again. My boys had drunk their meals and my Japan trip was a financial flop.

"Please forward me enough transportation money to get us back home," was the wire I sent Demon Hyde. He answered promptly with enough extra money to pay the hotel bill. At least I wasn't in jail. We boarded the ship with third class tickets but the musicians used their cabins only to store their instruments and change clothes in, so actually that didn't make any difference.

Two Hollywood comedians were aboard, the famous Robert Woolsey and Bert Wheeler. It didn't take long for us to get acquainted, since I was in show business. We stood around the piano singing, telling smutty stories and in general raising old Ned. The community was out in full force in Shanghai to greet them and us when we arrived and at the Cathay Hotel some one presented Bob Woolsey with a small table radio. A little later when we were all in their apartment I suggested a little music. Woolsey asked me would it be all right to play the radio, I said, "Sure, Bob, why not?" He plugged it in and it blew up in his face. The current in Shanghai is 220-V and this was an American radio 110-V. if looks could kill, I would be buried.

In trying to square myself, I got carried away and invited Bert and Bob to dinner at the famous Little Club. Of course, I had only three hundred fifty Shanghai dollars left, which was roughly seventy U.S. dollars, and that was part of what I received from

Demon Hyde. I almost fell off my chair when the two comedians showed up with twelve uninvited guests.

The party started out with cocktails and later we had champagne. Lots of it! It sounded like the fourth of July the way the corks were popping. It was gala as could be, but I couldn't eat or drink from worrying about the bill. The way things were going, it looked to me like I'd have to wash dishes for a year.

I kept bothering the head waiter for a running account of the tab and when he told me that we had passed the twelve hundred mark, I got dizzy. Then somebody ordered more champagne and I didn't know whether to walk out or just quietly lie down under the table.

After a couple more bottles of bubble water, someone tapped me on the shoulder and when I looked around it was the owner, Mr. Monty Berg. I knew that the time had come. But what does he say – "Whitey, it was wonderful of you to bring Wheeler and Woolsey to my club for their first party. Everything is on the house."

"Waiter! More champagne!"

21

IN ADDITION TO WAR and curfew, the 1933 depression was felt in Shanghai, and things were pretty tough. I wasn't doing so well and had a lot of time on my hands. During the day, I would drop in at the Palace Hotel bar to see my friend Tug Wilson, the manager, and chew the rag. For a while nearly every day a character came in looking for Julian, the bogus oil promoter, who was hiding out in Shanghai from the law. This guy told Tug that he had a secret formula for synthetic gasoline which had been given to him by an old German friend who had died. He called it Zerolene. Tug asked me if I was interested and I told him that I wanted no part of it. The guy kept coming back and Tug asked me again if I wanted an introduction. I told him no again, Tug looked at me and said, "Whitey, wouldn't it be funny if a million bucks was walking right by your nose? And you're saying no!"

I always was a sucker for a million dollars and told Tug OK, bring him over. His name was Harry Bowerman and just like he had rehearsed the act a hundred times, he took a small bottle from his pocket and poured some of the contents into an ash tray and put a match to it. The explosion almost blew the roof off and I was sold. Harry told me that the basis for this synthetic gas was alcohol, and that the rice hulls that the Chinese farmers were burning up or burying in the ground showed bigger percentage of alcohol than any other raw material.

Hook, line and sinker! Everything looks like a silver dollar! This time I'm going to make a million for sure! I told him I could

I DIDN'T MAKE A MILLION

promote the set-up he wanted providing that he made a test. And I told him that if he asked for any money before he poured the finished product into the car and it chugged off, I would know he was a phoney. He agreed.

I arranged for the test-chemists, lawyers, machinists, newspapermen – and Swan Culbertson and Fritz to finance the deal. I rented an old soap factory and had rice hulls delivered to the yard until it looked like the Swiss Alps. The Associated Press picked up the story and it was on the front page. I could see the future headlines, "Band Leader Becomes Gasoline King of China" – "Standard Oil and Shell Worried" – "Oil Companies Offer Band Leader Top Job."

Came the day for the big show. On our arrival the factory was crowded, and right at the start they were asking me how I wanted the boilers hooked up and the pipes to run. I looked around for my angel. I found him out on the street walking up and down kicking horse eggs. I asked him to come in and show the engineers what he wanted. Oh, he said, that wasn't what was worrying him. I was nervous and told him if it was money all he had to do was make the stuff and when the car ran I would hand him fifty thousand dollars good will money.

No, he said, there were too many people around and he couldn't take a chance on someone discovering his secret. I told him that I would ask them to leave. "No," he said , "Let it go until tomorrow." –

The next day it was the same thing. The executives questioned me and when I looked for my Zerolene partner he's sitting in back of my car. By this time I was a little peeved and said, "Come in and show them how you want to do this miracle." He said that he must go back down to his hotel, that he forgot some of his secret formula, so I told him to hurry and said that I would hold the big shots until he returned. We waited and waited and

WHITEY SMITH

then everybody left. I went down to Brownie's Bar on Broadway where Harry hung out. I asked the bar manager if he had seen or heard anything of my running gas head. He said sure, he was just here and told me that he wasn't going on with the test unless he got five thousand dollars in advance. Just then Harry came in and I asked him why he didn't come back, trying to hold my temper. When he said he wanted five thousand dollars before starting, he broke his agreement and I almost broke his jaw. He was stretched on the bar room floor and I stepped over the body to the bar and had a double scotch. He got up after a while, shook himself, then pointing at me and shouted, "Whitey Smith! You just missed making a million dollars."

My angel with the black wings was all booked up for a job on a freighter and left early the next morning.

Years later I met Mr. L. K. Taylor, who was one of the interested parties. He told me that this phoney was right in one thing and that was the alcohol in the rice hulls. He said they had incorporated and established a distillery, making Dominion Scotch out of rice alcohol.

I was busted and had moved out into the French Concession, hybernating in an attic room of a cheap boarding house. I couldn't even pay my rent there and before long the German landlady told me one morning that if I didn't pay the hundred Shanghai dollars I owed by nightfall, I would have to move.

I started out looking for someone who could give me a helping hand. It was raining black cats and blue dogs and things looked mighty dark for Whitey Smith. I was just about to the point of contemplating the easiest way to start a crap game when I passed the entrance of the Palace Hotel bar. Some friend had told me that there was a fellow inside raising hell because no one could tell him where he could find Whitey Smith.

I asked him if he knew who this man was. No, he didn't,

but he said that the guy looked kind of odd and was wearing a derby hat. Oh, yes, he heard him say something about oil. Then I remembered, that the *President Coolidge* had docked that morning and sure enough as I slipped up to the door and peeked, there was my Burma oil friend, Joe Grove!

I walked in and Joe made a run for me, put his arms around me and asked why the heck is it no one could tell him where I lived.

Not wanting to admit my circumstances I told Joe that I was doing fine and was building a new home out in French town which I hadn't told anyone about. Joe wasn't convinced and over and over asked if I needed anything. And over and over I told him, no, not a thing.

The more we drank the soberer I got, because I kept thinking about the rent I had to get before nightfall. "You're not the same Whitey Smith I met in 1928. Something is worrying you."

He reached over and put five hundred dollars American in my pocket. By this time Joe had had many drinks, so I gave it back to him saying that I didn't need it.

"Whitey", he said, "I've got nine thousand dollars on the Coolidge, but I'm not staying here this time, and if you don't tell me now what you need before we pull out, it will be too late."

For some reason I couldn't bring myself to tell him about my troubles so we went from place to place through the day into the night. At every stop Joe would pay the bill in American dollars and get Shanghai dollars in change. He would just crumple it up and stick it in his pocket. That went on all night and by morning his pockets were bulging with Shanghai money.

When it was time for Joe to go aboard his liner he remembered his watch which he had put in a repair shop when he arrived. By then it was too late to pick it up so I told Joe that I would pick it up for him and in the meantime he could have my watch.

WHITEY SMITH

Joe said, "Whitey, mine is only a cheap thing, and yours with that Masonic diamond fob is too fancy for me." But I talked him into it and we shook hands. I told him if we ever see each other again we will change back our watches.

As Joe walked up the gangplank, he turned, and said, "Wait a minute, Whitey," and he dug into his pockets and pulled out his Shanghai dollars which he had received in change and made a ball out of them. He took aim and threw it to me, shouting, "I can't spend this in San Francisco."

There I had been looking for a hundred, and when I got back to the bar for a quick one and counted the ball of money, I had forty-five hundred! Bread on the water. I went home and paid the back rent and moved into the best hotel in Shanghai with all the trimmings.

But everything I touched turned to mud and I couldn't seem to make any kind of a deal, even with Joe's stake. Finally, Mr. Henry Adams asked me to take my band to the Edgewater Mansion Hotel, which was a summer resort that he was opening in Tsingtao up the coast from Shanghai. He was the manager of it. I didn't see how a summer resort that far away during a time of world depression could make a go of it, but who was I to worry about that. At least I had a job for my boys and me. Mr. Adams gave me a cash advance to get the boys up there and once again Whitey Smith was on the way.

I made a bad start. The night before we left for Tsingtao I lost the transportation money on Jai Alai. But, naturally, I didn't say anything to the band about it. We were traveling by Japanese ship and someone told us not to worry, for he thought that I could pay the fares at the other end. That was also a gamble.

We boarded and the musicians stacked their instruments in a pile on the main deck. After the ship was on its way, the Japanese purser began picking up the tickets. When he approached the men in the band, they referred him to Mr. Whitey Smith, their band leader. But he couldn't find me since I was hiding down below biding time until the ship was too far out to make us swim back.

I heard some of the boys' wives crying so I showed myself. The Japanese officers surrounded me.

"Tickets, prees-s-s-s." The Japs always hiss. They think it is polite. I gave them a couple of sick "heh, heh's" and said, "I've made arrangements for the manager of the hotel to meet us when we arrive and he will pay for our tickets then."

"Oh. very sorree, must have tickets now."

"Well, I'm sorry too, but the fares will be paid when we get there."

The Japs didn't think much of that and rushed me to the office where there was a big discussion of what they were going to do with me. They decided to lock me up. So they did. The Japs have a reputation for being clean, but it wasn't established through their brigs.

While I was sitting among the filth I thought suddenly of my four months at Camp Lewis. With this I called for the captain and said, "Sir, I'm an American war veteran," and, getting carried away, "Like our first President, George Washington, I cannot tell a lie." This was irrelevant but I continued, "On the upper deck we have five thousand dollars worth of instruments. You may select any one you like to keep in your office until the transportation is paid. Just let me out of here."

After an inspection and much consultation, they selected the biggest instrument in the lot, the Sousaphone, for security. They were happy; I was happy; the only one who was not happy was the Sousaphone player and he sulked the whole voyage.

I wired Mr. Adams, and he met us at the dock with an advance. The Japanese released the big horn and the bass player

WHITEY SMITH

was happy again.

"This Edgewater Mansion promotion was another white elephant and caused a run on the Bank of Tsingtao, which closed with a loud crash. The hotel was too modern and too big for a resort season of two months a year. After our contract expired we returned to Shanghai. Things were breaking bad. I released the band and went to work at the New Paramount night club as master of ceremonies. My only compensation for this was meeting a charming girl one night through a friend of mine. I knew that I had met the woman in my life. Not being smart enough to get her address, the next day I had to find her. I couldn't eat or sleep, a malady loosely associated with love and poverty. I found out later, as I suspected, I was in love. When I caught up with Helen I found she felt the same way about it. Among the things we had in common was bustedness. But we walked on a cloud.

To keep from starving I agreed to go to Chefoo for Jimmy James, well-known in Shanghai for his Jimmy's Kitchen. He was opening a place there called the St. George's. I didn't have enough money to pay my room rent and until it was paid, couldn't move my instruments. Helen came to my rescue. Frugally she had saved her rent which wasn't due until the end of the month and I borrowed it until I got my advance.

22

I BROUGHT A four-piece combo along with me to Chefoo and Jimmy sent eighteen girls of all creeds and nationalities. The St. George's did a humdinger of a business. Chefoo being a U.S. naval base we depended strictly on the white hats until eleven o'clock when liberty was up. Then the officers came after getting a head start at their club – some with their wives, some without their wives, some with somebody else's wife.

Later Helen came to Chefoo and worked as a featured dancer at the Beach Cafe, my competition. She did her dance routine twice a night and usually would finish early. She came to the St. George's until I was finished and then we would sit and moon like a couple of half-baked kids and hold hands until daylight and then go swimming. What a beautiful summer.

When it was time for Jimmy James and me to settle our business I was told that we would settle on our return to Shanghai and he handed me a third class ticket on a coal ship. Helen gave up her job and came along. To be honest that was a dirty, black trip. Five minutes out we looked like Al Jolson singing Mammy.

Back in Shanghai Jimmy stalled me off until I started with my band at his club there, also called the St. George's. To help settle his account with me, Jimmy took me to his tailor where I could order some new clothes and he could sign for them. His credit was good all over the city. He asked me if I would like to have a radio and I said I would. But there still was a balance. The Shanghai St. George's was a success because the band was pulling them in. We were on the air every night since Jimmy had his own radio station, RUOK.

The Paramount Night Club people asked me to move my band over to their place and as Jimmy and I couldn't see eye to eye about many things, I accepted the offer. I settled the balance of my Chefoo business with Jimmy by accepting his speaker and amplifier system.

We did well at the Paramount, but there was talk of war with Japan and everybody, including Whitey Smith, had the jitters. Helen told me that she had an offer to go with a show to Manila to play at the Manila Hotel and I told her to grab it because it would give her a chance to look over possibilities for the future for both of us.

I dug up some dough and opened the Little Club at Chefoo. The club was a small one that could accommodate about fifty or sixty people. I had a four-piece combo, all Americans and twenty-two hostesses: mostly Russian girls from Shanghai. Everything started out with a bang-and everybody told me that I was sure to make a million.

I had my troubles with the Navy. Big Dutch, the baker on the *USS Black Hawk*, always came ashore with a chip on his shoulder. One Saturday night this Dutchman came into my Little Club by himself, and sat down across from a sailor off the same ship. The music played to a packed club and they just sat and "dog-eyed" each other. After a while the Black Hawk baker stood up, walked around the table, picked up his shipmate by the middy and hit him square on the button.

The Black Hawk crew, present in force, joined in and everybody was fighting, but no one knew what about. The Dutchman was shouting to me not to interfere, and told me to keep out of the way.

Dutch had flattened five or six of his buddies by the time the

I DIDN'T MAKE A MILLION

Navy shore patrol arrived and arrested the cake maker.

The next morning Dutch was up for court martial and the patrol officer came after me to appear as a witness and to make a charge, but I refused. Dutch was found guilty anyway and was sentenced to thirty days in the brig.

On his release Dutch looked me up with the idea of pinning my ears back, saying I was the one who had him pinched. Without waiting for an explanation, he wrecked my Little Club, breaking tables and chairs, with special emphasis on glasses. He ruined my business for the night, to put it mildly. Afterward the Dutchman pushed me into the nearest bar, bought me a drink and said, "Whitey, you know I wouldn't start trouble in your joint. You're my pal!"

Whenever one ship had a grudge against another ship, there was danger in the air and on payday the Little Club was filled to the doors. On one such night a party of "White hats" from the destroyer *Parrot* sat on one side of the club across from a party from the destroyer *Perry*. Wise cracks were being cast from side to side and I figured this riot should be held some place else. But I had to hurry, so I called Bo'sun's Mate Tom Ponder from the Perry.

I asked Tom if trouble was coming and he told me, "Whitey, you don't know what trouble is until this one starts. We're going to teach that Parrot gang to keep out of our way and it may start any minute." So I asked Tom to take it to the competition next door, commonly referred to as "Smells Bad".

"Okay, Whitey," he said, 'I'll take it next door to Smells Bad, but when we leave, you tell the Parrot where we are." I agreed and the Perry crew left.

In a few minutes I heard a loud crash. The street was crowded with fighting sailors and the shore patrol was dragging the boys to the paddy wagon. Smells Bad now looked bad.

Even the girls got into the act when it came to brawls in Chefoo. During the summer when the Navy held maneuvers near this little Chinese village, some of the men would bring their American wives with them from Shanghai. It was a kind of resort. But the number of American women compared with the total number of American sailors was indeed few. So at night they would all come to my Little Club for gaiety. The sailors took turns dancing with their buddies' wives.

This seemed to work out okay until one night one of the husbands, a big strapping machinist's mate, slipped across the room while his wife was dancing with one of his friends and asked Shanghai Mary, one of the Chinese hostesses, to take a turn around the floor. When the dance was over, the machinist mate's wife, "Little Dempsey", as they called her, walked over and threw twenty cents into Mary's face. Mary didn't care much for this and threw the money back. Little Dempsey retaliated with a right cross to the jaw, which made Mary's sister, Lily, think she should do something, so she threw a chair. Some of the sailors tried to break it up and the hostesses began to throw everything that wasn't tied down. Soon the sailors began to fight among themselves and finally I became referee. The decision? Loser: Whitey Smith. Joint wrecked.

One night when the Little Club was really jumping a flash came over the air, "Shanghai Bombed Thousands killed."

It was 1937, Bloody Saturday. Some scared Chinese pilot started out to drop bombs on the Japanese warships which were lying in the Whangpoo River. The Jap planes went up to meet him and the Chinese ran like heck. To pick up speed he tried to drop his load on the Race Track but missed. The bombs landed on Nanking Road, in front of the Cathay Hotel, and on Avenue Edward the Seventh, across from the track. Right away the U.

I DIDN'T MAKE A MILLION

S. Asiatic Fleet pulled out of Chefoo, lock, stock and barrel. The real war with Japan was just around the corner, and we knew it.

Well, there I am with twenty-two Russian girls and a band, plus wives, to feed and nothing coming in. I depended entirely on the Navy, since Chefoo is just a small city and a very native one at that. So now I was in trouble and dubious about making a go of it – out of cash, credit running out, and twenty-two Russian girls crying on my shoulder about how bad off their relatives are. The Navy had pulled out so quickly that I was left with a stack of unpaid chits a mile high.

I held on for a couple of months. One day I received a letter from Helen. She told me, "Darling, come to Manila. Everybody here knows you and anyway it's better to be in Manila than Shanghai in case of war. The Americans are here."

She was right. But how was I going to get there? I was broke as a hobo and worried about my obligations. That night I walked up and down the dark streets of Chefoo, looking up at the sky, praying for guidance, then went home to sleep.

My prayer was answered. The American Consul notified me the next day that the Americans would be evacuated and that I had my choice of going home to the United States or to Manila. I said I'd take Manila. I was to leave on the transport *U.S.S. Chaumont* in one week, but I couldn't go unless someone took over my outstanding debts and the responsibility of the girls and the business. The logical prospect was Jimmy James. I knew he didn't like my competition. So I made him a proposition.

"Jimmy, old pal, give me fifteen dollars and take over my obligations and you can have the Little Club." Jimmy agreed and I was on my way to Manila. The trip was to take ten days and I was billeted in what they said was the Chief's quarters. After we passed Shanghai I received an envelope and in it was a twenty dollar bill. The note read, "from a friend". I found out that it came from Mr. Chuck Culbertson of the Shanghai Brokerage Firm, Swan, Culbertson and Fritz. I've been looking for him ever since.

As we were approaching Hong Kong a typhoon was in the air and we couldn't land. I had planned on dropping in on my old company, the Hong Kong Shanghai Hotels, to see if I could interest them in booking me there. But I couldn't get ashore. I felt lower than a whale's tail.

I was sitting down in my quarters brooding and feeling the world was against me when someone called and said, "Whitey, the destroyer *Perry* is laying next to us and the commander says he wants to see you."

I got up there fast. The commander waved to me and then picked up a big megaphone and shouted up at me, "Whitey, how much do I owe you?"

I said I didn't know.

"I think it's fifty-three dollars."

"Fine," I replied, and he picked up an empty tomato can and stuffed it with money and threw it up to me. I emptied it and threw it back. A lieutenant returned it with more money in it and shouted, "Whitey, is that right? Thirty-two dollars?"

The can travelled back and forth until the last seaman who owed me dough had settled up. Then the commander took hold of the megaphone again and asked me, "What have you got to read?" and threw up a bundle of late magazines.

The chief steward, named O'Brien, took the meg and wanted to know if I had anything to drink. It is understood that on a Navy ship there is no liquor, but up came six cans of beer.

After leaving Hong Kong the executive officer of my ship called me up to his quarters. "Who the hell are you anyway?" he asked. I told him that I had been a night club owner in Chefoo and that some of the Perry's men had signed chits there, but had to pull out on an alert.

"Well!" he said, "Mr. Smith, I have never seen anything like it in all my experience. Talk about luck. Those men just got paid twenty minutes ago."

23

THE DESTROYER PERRY'S PAY call just before Hong Kong saved me from arriving in Manila broke. I had a pocket full of dollars and when I walked down the gangplank Helen was there, all smiles even though she had suffered influenza and had just gotten out of a sick bed.

It didn't take me long to see the manager of the Manila Hotel, Mr. Andy Anderson. He knew me by reputation and had requested me to come to the hotel three years ago. Mr. Anderson wanted to know if I could act as master of ceremonies for room and board and enough for spending money. I told him yes, sir!

Helen opened a dancing studio, but it didn't do too well and I couldn't stay satisfied forever with room and board, so I organized a band of Filipino musicians, and thereupon became acquainted with, "Filipino time". When I called a rehearsal for nine o'clock, I was the only one there at nine. The men would trickle in an hour or two later and think nothing of it, so we usually finished rehearsals before we started. But the boys could play.

One of my first jobs was a one-night stand at a political fiesta in the province of Tarlac. We had bargained on the price for a week. When we arrived the committee showed me where we were going to play and I wished that they hadn't. On a tennis court, a temporary bandstand had been built out of bamboo. It stuck up in the air about ten feet. There was a slant to it and it appeared ready to topple over any minute. There was no way

I DIDN'T MAKE A MILLION

that I could see to get up on it. They forgot to build steps.

After much agitation on my part, the committee got busy and built a ladder. But naturally there was no piano. When my sixteen men ascended to the top one by one the stand looked like the leaning tower of Pisa. All night I waited for the crash.

We were playing our first number when I noticed another band getting ready to play at the other end of the court. I didn't know that we had entered a "battle of music". The crowd yelled for their local band, and I'll have to admit, they were very good on their novelty numbers and their uniforms were flashy. I was trapped into a contest.

By now the "leaning tower" was creaking and felt like it was about ready to go all the way. My band was sitting like surveyor's plumbs so they could balance their weight.

The other outfit was making me look silly, playing all the Filipino songs for dancing. I remembered that I had some of my Chinese music with me, with words in English but which sounded like Chinese singing, and handed it out to the boys. That apparently was the answer because the crowd started laughing and applauding. We had the other gang stumped and won that battle.

As we played "Mabuhay" to end the evening, I saw the dance committee moving a big table out in the center of the court. They counted the take and paid us in one peso bills while everybody watched. The payoff was the high point of the evening. It always is to me.

Next I contracted the best job I could get, which was Ed Mitchell's Rhonda Grill. I gave the band a pep talk and I told them that if they listened to me we would become popular and then could demand more money.

On opening night the place was packed. After we had been on the job for an hour the band took a siesta, job or no job. I asked the piano player if he would play a little theme between dancing and he said he couldn't because he had to sleep. The hardest job I had with this band was waking them up before each set, then when I got them on the bandstand they would doze off in the middle of an arrangement.

I noticed night in and night out that I didn't see any uniforms – no sailors, soldiers or marines. I couldn't figure it out so after work one night I asked the club manager why we weren't getting any of the military trade and he told me that the place was off limits. Maybe I could get used to the inbetween siesta by the boys in the band, but when Tom King told me that we were off limits to the armed forces, I told him that I was off limits to the Rhonda Grill and I gave the band notice to do their sleeping at home.

This set-back discouraged me so much that I wanted to return to Shanghai, war or no war, so I went to see my friend Irving Ross, our American vice consul. He was real stern and told me, "Whitey, you arrived here at the expense of Uncle Sam and now you're asking to go back to Shanghai. What do you think your Uncle is, a free travel bureau?" I returned to my hotel room to sit and think.

Helen was working during the annual Manila Carnival in a show with a group from Shanghai. Never let it be said that she was afraid of work. One Saturday, Helen got the idea that maybe if she had a sewing machine she could mend costumes for the local vaudevillians and we in turn could eat. But she needed ten pesos for a down payment. So I looked up a friend, George Vogel, and I had ten.

The next day was race day and right across the street they were selling doubles tickets. I suggested to Helen that we should get just one ticket.

I didn't know one horse from the other , so I selected one named "No Chance", which was number seven. I didn't bother

I DIDN'T MAKE A MILLION

to look at the entries in the next race. I just said give me number nine. So there we were with tickets seven and nine.

Next morning we took a carromata for the track. Just before the race started we used our last sou for a hot dog sandwhich. It meant walk back if seven and nine didn't cross the border in time.

I couldn't sell this to Hollywood, but number seven won in the stretch, just like a girdle. All we had to do now was win the next one. Helen and I were pretty excited so we went over to the paddock to take a look at number nine. There were eighteen horses in the race and number nine was so small we couldn't find him. When finally we did, he looked like a donkey.

The second race was short. We never did see our horse, but some of the shouting was "number nine."

Hollywood wouldn't buy this one either. Helen and I just stood there looking at each other, afraid to peek at the board. When we did it said, "photo finish." There was still hope. The touts told us it would pay four hundred forty-six pesos. After a generation's wait, the board came up slowly and the shouting started. When we opened both eyes and saw that wonderful number nine, we were so happy that we gave what seemed most of it to the chiselers and touts before we could leave the window.

The king and queen of Manila were in the chips. Nothing but the best that night for Helen and my friend George Vogel – dinner, with champagne, at Tom Dixie's. To hell with the sewing machine.

I had my eye on a place where I could open a night club, but the old German owner wanted seventy thousand pesos, I was told. Helen picked up a deck of cards and told my fortune, which I didn't believe, but I grew hopeful anyhow when she pointed to a card and said, "That card means money. There will be an old gentleman calling on you who will change everything. He will

WHITEY SMITH

have for you what you are looking for."

I was a little peeved at Helen for building up what I thought were false hopes and stalked out. But when I walked through the lobby of a hotel next day I heard the call of the Philippines,"sssst," then someone said in a voice so guttural it rattled," Come he-ah just a minute, I would like to speak mitt Witey Schmitts. My name is Mathias Kraut. I have a r-r-restaurant and night club in the Metr-r-r-ropolitan Theater Building. Everybody tells me. you are de man. Vy don't you take my place? I vill make you de partner."

To make a long story short, I told him that I would need two thousand pesos to start with and he said, "Vot! You don't need any money. Everybody know you. Here's de key. You vill find liquor in das basement." It was almost as simple as that.

So I had the same place, for which I would have had to pay seventy thousand pesos, for nothing ... the Metro Garden and Grill. But I still had the problem of raising enough money to get myself a suit. The collar of my coat and the seat of my pants looked like they had been in a cat fight so I went to Mr. Kraut and asked him if he would lend me twenty pesos for a new attire. After having given me half interest on a seventy thousand pesos endeavor, his reply to my request for twenty pesos operating capital was, "Vot are you going to do mitt it?"

After a closer look and some consideration he gave it to me.

I bought a linen suit which cost eleven pesos and the remainder I spent for wire so I could lower the Metro's ceiling and hang numbers for spot prizes. I bought a few dozen Popeye the Sailor plastic dolls to give away. On hope I hired a ten-piece swing band, a four-piece Hawaiian band to alternate, hostesses, waiters and waitresses. Helen worked for me, doubting if she would get paid.

Three sleepless nights before the opening I recalled that the

I DIDN'T MAKE A MILLION

Asiatic Fleet had just pulled into Manila Bay with seventeen ships and that they would get paid on November fifteenth, my opening night. I sat down immediately and wrote a letter in my best block print to the commander of each of the seventeen ships asking him if he would let me renew old acquaintances by posting my letter on the board so the men would know that I was opening the Metro Garden. I added an obvious come-on, "P.S. Commander, would you drop in and have a drink with me?"

With the crowd I got, you would have thought that it was New Year's Eve. To begin with, I had no change so I borrowed fifty pesos for one hour from the first sailor that walked in. At twelve o'clock my bartender told me we had no more beer or whisky, and me with a full house! We did, however, have plenty of Rhine wines, so I stepped on the bandstand, took the mike and said, "Fellows, this is my first night in operation here. I have run out of hard liquor. I would appreciate it if you would stick around and have some of my German Rhine wines and some liqueurs stored in the celler. Just ask the waiters and waitresses what I have. Thanks. "

I didn't lose a customer. And I was in business again.

For quite some time I had been unable to send help to my parents in the States but now that the Metro Garden was going good, maybe I could begin again to contribute. Word came that my mother was ill with that dreaded disease, cancer.

Christmas was just a week off and I thought that this would be her last, so I wrote a letter in a hurry, put some money in the envelope, and ran over to the post office to make the last air mail before the holidays. Just as I got to the window it closed in my face. I hurried to the Manila Hotel branch, praying that I would make it. Closed!

Then I rushed to the dining room where the airline crew members were having their dinner. I told the officer in command that if this letter didn't get on this plane my mother wouldn't get it for her last Christmas.

"I'm sorry," he said, "but that is against regulations."

I ran to the Pan American office. The young lady in charge said she was sorry, but that there might be a chance if I went up in back of the post office and caught them while loading the sacks.

Sure enough, they were putting the mail in the truck. I asked for the man in charge and the Filipino gentleman listened to me.

"This letter is for my mother who is very sick," I pleaded. "If I can get it in this mail, she will get it for Christmas."

The Lord must have heard my prayer. This wonderful Filipino, God bless him, reached down, took a sack and broke the seal, stamped my letter, stuck it in the sack, shook my hand and said, "Your mother will receive your letter on Christmas." She did, and it *was* her last Christmas.

24

WHEN THE FLEET left Manila for maneuvers it was a struggle to hold on, but upon the sailors' return it was clear going. In 1939, finally, I became solvent enough to feel that I could afford to get married. I was pretty sure of myself so I got the ring before I asked Helen.

I told her I thought she was the most wonderful girl I ever knew. She gave me that look and said tell me more. So I said let's get married.

This must have sounded all right because she accepted me. We hopped in a taxi, took along a couple of friends to act as witnesses and looked up a judge. We were very happy. Helen arranged our own home, we had our own car and the beginning of a bank account, and the Metro Garden was more popular every day.

One day a gentleman by the name of Bill Barnum, representing Pabst Beer, offered me the company's radio program for the Philippines, a half hour program, three nights a week. I featured the show from the Metro with our twelve-piece band and a Hawaiian quartet. The most popular part of the show was "I Heard" where I talked for a quarter of an hour on news and gossip.

I had always been interested in sports and we had some of the best talent in the world come through Manila. The heroes of the ring drew enormous crowds at exhibition fights. I knew the promoters and they often called on me to manage the

WHITEY SMITH

introductions. In 1939, I introduced Jack Dempsey from the center of the ring to a crowd of sixty thousand. Later on, it was Joe Louis and still later Rocky Marciano, who drew a hundred thousand.

When Joe Louis came through he spent his spare time knocking a golf ball around. Joe was pretty good, playing in the eighties. He was accustomed to playing without a hat, so one day I undertook to give him some advice. I told him I knew he had been hit hard during his career in the ring, but that he probably didn't know what a wallop the tropical sunshine packed when you went around a golf course in the middle of the day without a hat.

"I know you're right, Mr. Whitey, but you know, I can't find a hat out here big enough for my head."

I told him I would take care of that and I got in my car and went hat hunting. I made the rounds of most of the sporting goods and hat stores. Surprising how hard it was to find big sizes. I picked up five or six different ones, all of which looked to me about ten-gallon capacity, and brought them to Joe's apartment, laying them on the table.

Joe stuck one on his head and looked in the mirror. He looked like the famous comedian, Bert Williams, with that little thing perched on top of him. The more hats he tried the funnier he looked, until he picked up the last one. It was a sombrero straw, made in the Philippines, with a green celluloid peak in front. "That's it," said Joe. "Just right."

The last I saw of that skimmer, it was in Joe's hand as he waved to the crowd on his takeoff for home, shouting "Mabuhay!"

We had the Pabst program until the war broke out. The Navy made the Metro its headquarters ashore and nightly there were three to four hundred white hats coming through the door. The men knew they would be taken care of when they were at the

I DIDN'T MAKE A MILLION

Metro Garden and they called me "the admiral ashore". I would listen to their troubles, which were many, and try to give them advice. When they needed ten, or had a thirst without money – Whitey was the admiral.

One time Mrs. Claire Booth Luce, wife of the 'Time Magazine publisher, visited Manila. She spent an hour or so watching the Asiatic Fleet in action at the Metro. I will never forget what she said:

"Look at this – these men haven't the least worry about war and yet it is so close. Look at them dancing and drinking with not a care." And that was the way it went along.

The U.S. army was represented in the Philippines in those days by the 31st Infantry, which was stationed nearby, but they couldn't afford to spend as much as the Navy, since then a soldier didn't get as much pay and he was ashore all the time. A 3lst doughboy would go out and buy a bottle of local sandpaper gin, which was very cheap, come in the Metro with it, hide it under the table, and order a bottle of coke. The soldier would take up my best table for hours, and then when he finished he was drunk enough to argue about his twenty centavo check. Then I had to telephone the Military Police.

What a thirst won't do in the army! One night, a fellow in civilian clothes stood at my bar door with a large camphor-wood chest on his shoulders. He asked if he could bring it in. I told him to come right in and asked him what he wanted.

"My name is George Johnson," he said, "I've just started working for Marsman and Co., and I don't get paid until the end of the month. I've got a wife and three kids, and I have to raise some dough to make ends meet. Could I leave this camphor chest with you for twenty pesos until then?"

Hell, standing in the doorway with this big trunk on his shoulder, he looked like one of the stevedores at the San Francisco docks, so I gave him the twenty, and I had myself a camphor chest. I've still got it.

It seems the boys had been sitting in their barracks broke, trying to think up a way to raise some dough. This fellow figured he could get some credit from the corner Chinese novelty shop by saying he would pay at the end of the month. So he took the most expensive thing the Chinaman had and signed a chit for fifty pesos. So the 31st Infantry went on the town that night. I got a bargain sale camphor chest and the Chinese got a chit.

But when the fleet was in, if there was anything that was plenty in Manila, it was white hats. We were so well off, as a matter of fact, Helen and I were contemplating a trip back to the good old United States.

Again I was just on the brink of real success when the Japanese got into the act and blasted Pearl Harbor. It was the 8th of December in Manila (the 7th in the U.S.) when we heard the flash that the Nips had struck.

I recall thinking at the time that finally it had happened. Years before, in Shanghai, it was common talk among the Americans and British and our Chinese friends that the Japs were going to one way or the other mix it up with America and anybody else, who got in their way. Even so far removed as we were from government and economics, it was obvious that the Japanese were trying to take over Asia. Further, in Manila some of the high ranking officers whom I knew on General MacArthur's staff and also staff officers from the Navy headquarters at Cavite had expressed great concern that there would be a war with Nippon.

There were a number of American businessmen in Manila who took it upon themselves to organize locally to provide protection such as air raid shelters and a place for internment for American citizens in the Philippines because they felt sure that there was going to be trouble. As I remember, Mr. Frederic

I DIDN'T MAKE A MILLION

H. Stevens was the chairman of that committee and a Lt. Colonel Robert M. Carswell acted as military advisor. They were not satisfied with the American high commissioner's policy in approaching the possibility of hostilities.

Actually, the attack was no surprise, but yet when it happened we couldn't believe it. Helen and I closed the Metro Garden and Grill that night and stayed in our residence, which was very close to Nichols Field (still so called by the Philippine Air Force). The next night Japanese bombers came from the north, bombing Nichols Field and shattering the windows in our home. Needless to say, this caused us to think seriously about moving.

The next morning Helen and I got into our 1940 Oldsmobile and drove over to the Manila Hotel to see if we could find someone to tell us what to do. We were standing in the doorway of the hotel when there was a Japanese air raid over the city again. When the all-clear sounded the man who had been standing shoulder to shoulder with us was General Douglas MacArthur. He stepped into his limousine, giving us a salute as he drove away. Helen and I went back to our car and started for somewhere, but we didn't know where.

My wife, always practical, suggested that we stop at the first grocery store and load up the car. This sounded good to me and we filled that beauty like it was a Mack truck and then we left.

At the time I didn't know it, but some vicious gossip started a rumor which connected me and my radio program with my silent German partner, Mr. Mathias Kraut. Whoever started this nonsense did a real good job because it traveled the world over and I heard it even after the war.

The rumor had it that I knew too much about the Navy and that on my radio broadcast I talked too much. My German partner, Mr. Kraut, was supposed to have been a Nazi and, therefore, so was I. After all, my name was Schmidt! Furthermore, somebody said, the United States Marines had gone into the office of the Metro Garden and Grill and shot both Helen and me. Somebody else said, that I had been taken to Corregidor and shot for treason.

Fortunately, neither Helen nor I knew anything about this terrible talk. We had our hands full just trying to get somewhere away from the war and if we had known about the talk that was going on, we certainly would not have left Manila and by that token we might not be alive today.

25

Helen and I didn't have any idea where we were going when we left Manila, but we took the South Road. Pretty soon we found ourselves in Los Banos, about forty-five or fifty miles from the city where there is an agricultural college belonging to the University of the Philippines. Some American Navy fellows were there with seven seaplanes which they had hidden on the nearby lake – Laguna de Bay.

They recognized me and the first thing they asked was if I had anything to drink. I gave them a couple of bottles of Canadian Club whisky and after a drink or two they asked where we were going to stay that night. I told them that across the lake seemed like a good place and we said goodbye and left.

We rented a small room in a cottage we found and settled ourselves for the night. Helen was preparing supper in the hallway when suddenly the little cottage was riddled by rifle and machine gun fire. We dropped to the floor like short cigarette butts and thought for sure that the whole Imperial Japanese Army had descended upon Whitey and Helen Smith. Why they would want us we couldn't understand, but as it turned out one of the Filipino houseboys was standing on the bed trying to adjust the bulb in the blackout shade, making the light blink on and off.

The sailors outside thought that the blinking was code signals that we were giving to the Japanese. So far as they were concerned, this added credence to the rumor that Whitey Smith was a Nazi spy. Of course, I didn't know what was going on at the time, so when the shouting quieted down we got the heck out of there as fast as we could. Next morning we found ourselves back in Los Banos.

We asked some people on a street corner where they would recommend us to hide out and they suggested that we go to the College of Forestry and seek out a Mr. Hugh Curran, who was chief of the forestry department.They gave us the direction and having no place else to go we headed for the college and found Professor Curran.

He didn't know exactly what to do himself. He thought like the rest of us that it was going to be a three-month war and Uncle Sam's troops would be back to liberate us. But soon we found out that the Japanese had by-passed Los Banos and that we were actually behind the lines. This was the deciding factor. We all agreed that we should take to the hills, leaving immediately, led by Mr. Curran and his wife in their truck.

Our destination was Mt. Makiling, accessible only by a zigzag road with heavy forest on each side. Mr. Curran and his truck got way ahead of us and the first thing we knew we were by ourselves again. I thought it was hopeless. I burned out the bearings in my car and with that I wanted to coast into a nearby Jap camp and surrender. But Helen would have none of that, so I coasted as far as I could safely and then turned off the road. A clump of bamboo trees stopped us. And there we were on New Year's Eve of 1942.

For five days and five nights we stayed in that spot, eating and sleeping in the car. Remember, we had loaded up the back end with all the groceries we could get. Each moment of our stay there was like waiting for the guillotine. Every movement of the tree leaves spelled danger to us and I could see a grinning Japanese face behind each tuft of grass.

On the fifth night Mr. Curran found us. He told us to pack

our stuff and led us over to the other side of the mountain where we joined his camp. He seemed confident we could all hold out there until the boys liberated us.

A few days later two American officers with eleven constabulary soldiers came into camp. The constabulary men had changed into civilian clothes and the two American officers had long beards and remnants of U. S. Army uniforms. They had two machine guns with plenty of ammunition and they set these guns up in our camp, telling us if the Japs attacked they would fight until death. Whose death, we wondered.

The next morning the constabulary men went to town to mingle with the people and that afternoon the officers somehow recognized the danger they had put us in and decided to head for Corregidor. Helen scrounged a couple of chickens and some other food and Mr. Curran drew them a rough map of the area. They were in the 31st Infantry and the two officers, having known me from the Metro Garden and Grill, bet me in all seriousness that they would be back in Manila in three months. I told them that I would give them each a case of champagne to celebrate. I haven't seen them since, but the offer of the champagne still stands.

We decided that the best thing for us to do now was to move to a new location, so the next morning at four o'clock we headed further over the mountains. Helen and Professor Curran took bolos and hacked out a place for us to stay. We moved seven times, always at night. Eventually we contacted college students who brought us food and we passed day after day in endless waiting. The food supply ran seriously short because the college students had become frightened. And as we expected, a runner came to us one day with a message from the dean of Los Banos college. It said that the Japanese captain in that sector knew where we were hiding and offered safe passage to Santo Tomas if we would surrender peacefully – and turn in our arms.

Professor Curran was ill with fever, having developed blood poisoning in a bruised hand. It really appeared senseless for us to resist any longer. We all talked it over and Mr. Curran agreed and the next morning we dug up the cigar box we had buried containing our private papers and in turn buried all of our valuables.

When we knew war was coming I had tried to figure some way of saving the Metro stake we had in the bank – the money we were going to use for a nice trip to the States – and decided, on good advice, to buy diamonds. They were universal currency, good any time, war or no war.

So I bought twenty thousand pesos' worth of diamonds (ten thousand dollars) and we had them with us. But we knew we wouldn't have them long if the Japs found us so Helen and I decided to bury them right there on the mountain' side and mark the spot so we could retrieve our little fortune if we got out of this thing alive.

She picked a spot beside a bamboo tree and buried her jewel case in the dirt. She placed a big stone on top of it and notched the bamboo so she would know the marks. Carefully she stepped off the distance from the trail and marked it in relation to other things around.

Just before we arrived in Los Banos and turned ourselves in, some American missionaries and priests, teachers at Los Banos college, had surrendered. They looked at our papers and then pushed us over with the missionaries.

While we were hiding in the mountains the termites had gone through our cigar box and its contents like a buzzsaw. I had been registered on my passport as a musician but the termites obligingly had eaten the entire word with the exception of the letter "m". To the Japs this meant missionary. Since Helen was my wife, she must be a missionary too. We boarded trucks and headed for Santo Tomas, the Japanese captain who had accepted our surrender riding behind us in a brand new stolen Packard.

We got as far as a small town called Calamba where the captain ordered a halt at his headquarters there. His soldiers brought me into his office and without further ado the captain hissed:

"You missionary, huh?"

I'm about as far from a missionary as you can get and still get credit at the corner drug store. But he insisted. I kept shaking my head no, but he couldn't understand English.

Finally in exasperation at my negative response he pulled out his Samurai sword and wiped it clean with his handkerchief. Then the big show-off took a hair out of his head to show me how sharp his weapon was. All this time he kept saying "missionary, ha," and then he would smile. I failed to see the humor of the situation.

Fortunately for me, the phone rang and the captain answered. Whoever was on the other end of the line got the captain all upset because after a shrill and lengthy conversation in Japanese he flung the phone across the room and stormed out of the office, motioning me to follow. I got back into the truck and we headed for Manila – and Santo Tomas.

The Japanese had nothing against the missionaries. In fact they treated them very well. The Jap captain just thought that I was lying.

26

So for the second time in my life, I was headed for jail. I guess I didn't tell about the first time. I never was proud of it, but it taught me a darn good lesson. I got to thinking about that on the ride from Los Banos up to Manila, where Santo Tomas was located. As I remember it I recited the story to Helen to sort of cheer her up. We were both low in spirits and pretty apprehensive as to what awaited us.

It was back in Oakland in the days when I was commencing to fight professionally and had to take odd jobs to keep the wolf from the door. This job was in the College Inn, a bar and billiard parlor where I was relief man for the pool ball racker. I got a dollar a night. The Inn was a meeting place for big shots in sports – fighters, jockeys, baseball and football players.

I saw people like Jim Jeffries, Ad Wolgast, Barney Oldfield, Tod Sloan, Eddie Miller, Frankie Burns, Battling Nelson and Jack Root. Jack Root was the light heavyweight contender of the world in 1908. The last time I saw him was in Shanghai during the twenties. If I remember right, he was a scout for a Hollywood movie studio, looking for a Chinese beauty to star in the movies. Jack always carried a mouthful of B-B shot which he expelled with a force and accuracy between his teeth. Believe me they hurt when they hit.

A special friend of mine (so I thought) was the cop on the beat. This bluecoat was friendly and we used to have a little conversation almost every night.

I DIDN'T MAKE A MILLION

One night as I was leaving the College Inn with my one smacker in my pocket, I stepped out of the door and shouted back to the bartender, that I was going across the street to play Chinese lottery with my day's earnings. And I did. Making my purchase, I stuffed all twenty of those five-cent tickets in my inside coat pocket. Of course, the game was illegal, so the Chinese proprietor gave his customers a cheap stogy when they left his joint so that it would look like you had gone in just to buy a cigar.

As I stepped out after buying the tickets a big flatfoot in a blue uniform touched me on the shoulder and said, "Whitey, take a walk with me and keep your hands out of your pockets." I was puffing on that cigar.

The bluecoat asked me what I was doing in that Chinese shop and I puffed faster and told him, I went in to buy a cigar. The further we walked the closer we got to the City Hall. I tried to get into my coat pocket, but as I'd get up there the copper would smack me over the knuckles with his night stick. I couldn't understand why this policeman was doing this to me since he was my buddy from the Inn. But tonight, he was all business.

I had cooked my own goose when I had shouted back to the bartender about playing lottery because this cop had been standing in a doorway nearby. When we arrived at the police station they searched me and, sure enough, there were the tickets – all twenty, with Chinese markings. But they didn't stop there. They found some dice, a deck of cards, some naughty pictures and some other things which a lad of my age probably should not have on his person. I was scared!

They took me up to the 13th floor. That's the lockup. Nobody knew of my predicament and I didn't know that I could ask to phone anyone. I was afraid to even open my mouth after taking one look at the jailer with the keys hanging on his belt.

WHITEY SMITH

They proceeded to strip me down and finding nothing more they threw me under a shower. That water was cold, thirteen floors up in the winter time. After that, I was marched to a concrete boudoir and locked up tighter than a drum. Come morning, they shoved at me something in a tin cup that looked like heavy oil. They said, it was coffee. And scraps from a loaf of stale black bread. Talk about Russia, this bread was so stale I couldn't bite through it. So, I used my fingers to dig in the middle and in doing so I got more on the floor than I did in my mouth.

Then I heard the key turn in the lock of my cell. But before I even could get out I got a slap on the ear. "Is that the way you live at home? Get down and clean them crumbs off the floor, you pig." I did, and we went downstairs.

Outside the judge's chambers I was lined up with drunks, vagrants, bums, robbers, nearly all with beards dirty gray, brown, black and red beards, some long, some short. All nationalities were represented. I felt pretty humiliated.

A plain clothes detective walked up and down the line. He recognized me from having seen me box and asked me what my offense was. I told him I had committed no offense, but I was there because I had played Chinese lottery. He said, that this was a very serious offense, but he would have a talk with the judge and ask him to make it easy for me.

He came back later with a worried look on his face and told me that the best he could do for me was six months. This judge was tough on Chinese lottery players, he said. And he walked away. I felt like I had just killed and eaten my grandmother.

On the witness stand was this big bluecoat buddy of mine, who, until last night, had always given me such a friendly smile. After the evidence was displayed I was called to the witness stand and asked if I plead guilty or not guilty.

"I'm guilty, Your Honor."

I DIDN'T MAKE A MILLION

The judge asked me if this was the first time that I had played Chinese lottery.

I said, "No, this is the first time I've been caught." Then he wanted to know if I had spent the night upstairs, and I replied, that I had.

"I'm going to let you off this time with a warning that should you ever come before this court again and be convicted of playing Chinese lottery, you will go to jail for a good long stretch. Prisoner released."

I walked out to the street in a trance feeling like an ex-convict and all I had done was play a game. I looked up and there was the police chief, Captain Bock. He asked me what I was doing there and I told him that I had been upstairs for playing Chinese lottery.

"Why didn't you phone for me downstairs?" he asked with a kind of funny grin on his face.

"They didn't tell me I could phone anybody, Captain Bock."

"Well, well, that's a shame, Whitey. If that ever happens again just give me a call."

"Captain, this will never happen again." It didn't, either. I quit my job at the College Inn and went back to my newspaper corner.

I have thought many times since that this was a pretty good way to handle anybody the cops thought was on the road to becoming a juvenile delinquent.

But Helen and I were not juveniles and our only delinquency in the eyes of our jailers was that I was an American and Helen was my wife. Helen, being a White Russian born in Harbin, Manchuria, could have been freed at the outset if she had agreed to swear allegiances to the Japanese Government. But she refused, saying she had married an American and that was where her loyalty lay. So we spent the next three years of our lives

WHITEY SMITH

in Santo Tomas Internment Camp as prisoners of the Japanese.

27

I WILL NOT attempt to give you a detailed account of our three years in Santo Tomas. There have been volumes written about it and I suspect there will be more. I'm not really sure if the true story of Santo Tomas will ever actually be told. There were up to seven thousand of us interned in various camps at one time, and I feel certain that you could get seven thousand different impressions if you were to take the pains to ask those who are still alive.

Santo Tomas is a Catholic university in Manila, founded in 1611 by Spanish Archbishop Miguel de Benavidez. It is in operation today and is reputed to have the finest medical school in the Philippines. The Japanese, according to information I gathered, had selected the University of Santo Tomas as an internment camp even before the American committee did. Actually, it was a logical choice because of location and facilities. It is in central Manila and has a large campus surrounded by a ten-foot stone wall. Needless to say, those of us who stayed there learned to hate it and I am to this day reluctant to approach its gates.

The first thing that impressed me upon my arrival as an internee was the fact that nobody spoke to me for a long, long time. Helen and I stood and sat outside somebody's office for hours on end. Finally, an interpreter came and without fanfare or preliminaries asked me one simple question, the answer to which apparently was to furnish the backbone for the dossier on Whitey and Helen Smith.

WHITEY SMITH

"What were you doing in the mountains?"

To me it was obvious, that we had been hiding out and the question seemed so silly that I felt like saying, "picking berries". But I thought better of that and wrote on the piece of paper he had given me, that we had left Manila to get away from the bombing, that someone had stolen my car and since the bridges were washed out, we couldn't get back. Then, for good measure, I added that I was not a missionary. Surprisingly enough, they accepted all this and then told Helen to sign some papers supporting the Japanese military and, being a Russian, she could leave. As I said, Helen turned this down flat and thereby became a guest of Emperor Hirohito.

After this, we filled out some more papers and accomplished a good deal of red tape. Just outside an American stopped me and for a moment he appeared to have seen a ghost. Then, he said, that I would really be surprised if I had heard what he had said about me the night before. I figured that I had just escaped having a Samurai sword thrust through my innards and statements of the previous evening were of little real importance to me. Nonetheless I said, "I would? What did you say about me?"

He proceeded to relate to me the story that was going around about my being shot for treason in Corregidor and so on. I worried about it, but I was not too concerned because I knew that the story was tommyrot. I was very much alive and I hadn't committed treason. I'll have to admit, however, that the atmosphere was a little cool toward me in Santo Tomas for a while.

Helen was placed in a room in the main building while I was taken to the Education Building and told, "Whitey, everybody works here." And they handed me a mop and a bucket.

If there is one thing I learned at Santo Tomas, it is how to clean a toilet. As a matter of fact, if I can ever get out of the night club business I'm going to hang up my shingle as a sanitation engineer. So far as the overall camp was concerned, I was a peon, but I was a king on the second floor of the Education Building. There wasn't a commode on the entire floor that wasn't under my direct, immediate and eagle-eyed supervision.

I must admit that at the beginning I was in charge of only one of the two latrines on my floor, but the Committee for Sanitation, recognizing my extreme aptitude for this kind of work and judging from my shiny results, called me before its members one day and promoted me to supervisor. This meant that now I had two latrines to clean instead of one. They were twelve-seaters.

Helen was assigned to such details as cleaning, cooking and gardening. After a couple of months, she suggested that we build a shack for us to live in. More and more people were coming into Santo Tomas by the day and with space becoming ever more critical, Helen figured that sooner or later the Japs would permit families to live in their own shacks. I laughed at her. Surely, we would be liberated very soon, even though I knew that Bataan and Singapore, and God knows what else, had fallen to the Japanese.

But Helen was determined; and with materials she picked up around the camp, begging, borrowing and scrounging, she built us a shack. And how right she was. Eighteen months after we had arrived at Santo Tomas the Japs gave their permission for married couple to live together and we moved in full time. Using a lot of foresight, Helen planted a small garden which we used as long as we could. Toward the end of internment, food was almost unheard of and I still remember how good those beans and peas from Helen's garden tasted before they gave out.

The first year actually was not too bad. We had adequate food and we were permitted to receive parcels from our Filipino

WHITEY SMITH

friends on the outside. Also, those who had money could send out and purchase on the open market. But this was stopped after the first year, because the food supply on the outside was diminishing and the strain put upon the Islands by the Japanese to feed their army was more than even the Japanese expected.

Our Central Committee, led at first by Mr. Earl Carroll, did a magnificent job of trying to provide us with food and other materials over and above what the Japanese furnished, but it could go only so far. A great amount of credit is due these people for the way they administered the camp. Earl Carroll, who was picked out of a lineup by the Japanese when they were first interned, headed the Central Committee for a year or so when the Japanese permitted a popular election.

Then the wand passed to Carroll C. Grinnell, who was head of General Electric in Manila before the war. He worked very hard at a thankless job, and the internees never knew how much they owed to his courageous and efficient administration. Later on I'll have a story to tell about Grinnell.

We had our own courts, our own police force and subcommittees and organizations to handle every phase of our lives. But always under the watchful and often cruel dictatorship of the Japanese. The head of our internee committee was the liaison man.

Things were awful at first while we were settling in. Nobody had anything to sleep on and darn little to eat. Everyone had been instructed on being brought into camp to carry just enough food for two or three days. That was a literal order, and the Japanese of course had provided nothing.

When we recovered from the initial shock of being in jail, things began to improve for a time as we were allowed to do things for ourselves like procuring food from "outside". We were all billeted in the various college classrooms and buildings, but

I DIDN'T MAKE A MILLION

gradually spread out around the campus in home-made shacks like the one Helen put together for us.

A lot could be said about the serious side of our internment, but I don't think this is the place to say it. There is no use bringing back unpleasant memories. What we all remember most is the things we laughed at. I was proud that all of us Americans, Englishmen, Dutchmen, Afro-Americans and the assorted enemies of the Japanese in wartime – with their women and children – could laugh and find things funny under such trying and chastening circumstances.

Please keep in mind, however, that I was the wielder of the plumber's baton on my floor in the Education Building and thereby due extra privileges such as getting up earlier in the morning than my companions so that I might have the "bawth" properly prepared.

As I said before, Helen had built us a shanty, as had many others, and we began to fan out. Soon there were enough shanties so that the entire area was divided into districts, each with a title like "Glamourville" and "Shantytown." These districts were governed like the boroughs of a city and every six months we had elections choosing our mayor, who in turn would represent us with the Internee Committee. This was a very democratic action and in most cases taken seriously.

I remember one election, when Mr. Oscar Rhorer was candidate for mayor in the district of "Froggy Bottom." During his campaign he would make stirring speeches and walk up and down between the shanties carrying a placard which said, "Vote For Rhorer for Mayor." Oscar won by a landslide. He was the only one running! Of course, Oscar made the inevitable statement that he would rather be a big frog in a small bottom, etc. . . .

Our camp shows were a very important morale factor. Most of them were produced by a showman I had met for the first time in 1934, when he was part of the Marcus show. He was Dave Harvey, who, with Danny Kaye, was the top feature in the Marcus production.

Dave built the stage at Santo Tomas and had costumes made out of whatever, rags he could dig up, besides taking care of such things as lighting, sound, music, etc. Of course, there were a lot of people who helped him, but Dave was the guiding light. He composed what I thought was a most appropriate theme song for our three years of education at the University of Santo Tomas, entitled, "Cheer Up! Everything's Going To Be Lousy."

Many of Dave Harvey's shows utilized the talent of one of our favorite internees whom we called Bumblebee, a three hundred pound (when he entered Santo Tomas) colored chap, who before the war ran a very fine restaurant. Bumblebee was a master trombone player and although he weighed only one hundred forty pounds when liberated he never lost his sense of humor or his ability to "slick out" the blues. One evening, I remember, Bumblebee brought all three thousand of his audience solemnly to their feet as he played the most beautiful and memorable rendition of "God Bless America" that I think anybody has ever heard. The Japanese were petty confused – the four guards sitting in the back stood up with us – and when the solo was over Bumblebee laid low for a few days fearing the Japs would catch on.

It was necessary for our Central Committee as well as the Japanese to institute certain rules and regulations for us to live by. One of these rules concerned drunkenness. Intoxication was one thing under the circumstances that could not be tolerated. However, there were people who came into our camp that had been drinking for years and years and were not about to stop imbibing just because somebody said so.

An example of this was my friend, a two hundred pound

Manila businessman whom we don't have to name. He was interned with a fifty-year thirst behind him and couldn't shut it off on such short notice. For the first year we were permitted to receive packages daily from our friends on the outside and among the items received every day by this gentleman was enough liquor to keep him walking in circles. He was picked up time after time.

Finally our intemperate friend was politely thrown into the camp clink, but he stayed drunker inside than he did outside. Nobody could figure out where he got his liquor. Walter Schoening, the jailer, was the only person authorized to bring his package from outside the gates while he was in jail, but Walt never found any bottles in evidence.

One day Walter discovered that the big melon-shaped papaya that he had been handing over each day with our friend's food was plugged and a bottle of rum had been emptied into it. He hadn't cared how long the war lasted until the morning he took a big slug out of his papaya and began coughing and spitting – the rum had been replaced with water!

28

MANY OF US IN Santo Tomas owed whatever small comfort we enjoyed to our Filipino friends on the outside. The Japanese during the first couple of years allowed them to bring in to us food, freshly laundered clothes, building materials for shacks, money and whatever small things they could smuggle in without detection. They risked their dignity and even their lives doing it. Many times, they were slapped around by Japanese guards as they waited in a long cue at the gate each morning. Some who came under suspicion were taken to Fort Santiago and never heard of again.

It was more than our small comforts that we owed to them. Many times it meant survival. They brought in hard-to-get medicines and special diet foods without which some of us would have died. Most of these loyal Filipinos were household help or personal friends or friends of friends on the outside. Their sacrifices cemented a personal bond between Filipinos and Americans and other foreigners which is indestructible to this day.

During the first year, I had gotten a message to Tom Pritchard, who owned the well-known Tom's Dixie Kitchen, that I needed fifty pesos. Tom, of course, obliged immediately and sent the money with a note in an envelope by Elino Flores.

Elino was a former lightweight champion of the Philippines and had fought the great Johnny Dundee for the world's lightweight title at Madison Square Garden in New York in 1923.

I DIDN'T MAKE A MILLION

Just before Pearl Harbor Elino was working for me as my head waiter and "chuck 'em out guy" when necessary. He was besides my employee, a very good personal friend.

At the front gate we all congregated at specified times each day to receive whatever our outside friends brought to us. They would lay the packages on a line and then the guard would call out the name of whoever the package was for and the owner would go forward and pick it up. There was a fifty-foot no man's land between the internees and the outsiders. When Elino arrived at the rope holding the outsiders back he spotted me on the other side and began waving an envelope at me. He was wearing large-sized dark glasses and had his hat down over his eyes.

I tried to signal him to cut it out and fall in line but he misunderstood and ducked under the rope and walked toward me. I stood behind the front line of internees and grabbed the letter over their shoulders and ducked because I knew what was coming. The Japs grabbed poor Elino and then tried to find to who the envelope was for. Sensing that all of us would be in a serious jam, Elino refused to divulge the addressee and from whom it had come. The brutal Japanese took Elino to the dreaded Fort Santiago prison and tortured him unbelievably. They executed such niceties as pounding bamboo slivers under his finger nails, kicking him in the groin, giving him the water cure, and generally mutilating his body with knives, bayonets, rifle butts, fists, and heavy boots until Elino was unrecognizable. But, he didn't sing.

It's lucky for Tom Pritchard and me that Elino didn't tell, because Tom had unwittingly written in his note that he was sorry that he couldn't do more than give me fifty pesos, but to keep my chin up because our boys were soon coming back, which at that time was treasonable talk to the Japanese. If they had read the letter, the three of us could have been beheaded.

Both Elino and Tom are in Manila today living comfortably as I am, thanks to the courage and loyalty of Elino Flores.

The Japanese were not all bad to us. There were exceptions. One hungry day a ten peso bill came into my hands through the line. My sister-in-law Galia, who was killed during the liberation, was working as a waitress in the Marfusha restaurant on Dewey Boulevard. Japanese officers frequently had their meals there. One evening she was talking to the proprietor, pleading for the next morning off so she could go to Santo Tomas and bring something to her sister and brother-in-law, Whitey Smith. One of the officers overheard and quietly approached her.

"Ah-h-h, so. You know Witty Smitsan. You do somesing for me? You give Witty this . . ." and he palmed a tenspot into her hand.

I got word to Galia to please thank him for me, whoever he was. She did, but apparently was not discreet enough about it. The officer looked daggers at her and shouted "Never hoppen, never hoppen!"

As he went out he turned and whispered to Galia, "Witty my friend in Tokyo." I never found out who he was.

In the month of February 1944 the Japanese closed off the front gate and forbade any more line and food packages. Up to that time, we understood our internment administration was under the Foreign Office in Tokyo. When the Japs commenced to lose the war they shifted the prison administration to the army, and things then got really tough. Our food ration went down to six hundred calories a day per person. They figure it takes twelve hundred to sustain life indefinitely.

One morning as I was working in my twelve-seater one of my helpers, Johnny Elam, brought me a hard boiled egg. I wanted to know where he got it and he said he found two over near the fence. Next morning the two of us were at the spot, hoping that Easter would come again, when a carretela passed on the outside and as it did so an elder Filipino man started throwing hard boiled eggs and small bread loaves over the fence. We were at the same spot every morning, but nothing happened for many days, and then again there was a downpour of hard boiled eggs. They couldn't have been for anyone in particular, for there were quite a few by now hanging around waiting for the eggfall.

One morning it was not only hard boiled eggs, there were a couple of roast ducks with the hard boiled eggs inside, and packages of native cigarettes. One of the cigarettes had been split open with no tobacco but a rolled-up note inside that said "Will come back." It was signed.

And he was back, but not throwing eggs. Tom Wolff, the owner of the Sanitary Steam Laundry was able to have one of his trucks come in with some provisions for the Red Cross and our benefactor jumped aboard like an employee with his pockets full of hard boiled eggs for Mr. Eric Westley (senior).

Day in and day out we were at the fence but no more Easter days came along.

After liberation, I found out that our Filipino friend was Santiago G. Bitanga, an executive in a rubber and plastic company in Manila.

Our Japanese jailers frowned upon love. Internment was a serious business and they didn't want anybody making a picnic out of it. The amount of cleverness and ingenuity that was exercised in order to snatch a moment of privacy was astonishing sometimes. Man and wife were not allowed to live together for a long time after the opening of the camp, and you would be surprised how important privacy became when you were interned and any day might be your last.

Our camp police were warned by the Japanese to be especially careful about infractions of the rules lest absolute segregation be imposed. They had to turn in a few violators just to keep the record clear. One particularly flagrant case came to trial in our little court and when the Japanese read the record they came up with a suggestion. They were really serious about it too.

Our friend Eddie Tait owned a circus and he found out that most of the trappings were intact. Among them was a very large tent which he had asked permission to bring into camp. Ah-h-, so. Very good-o. We would set up the tent for community lovemaking purposes, all supervised, shipshape and aboveboard. There would be partitions inside and the line of couples would form at the left and take turns.

Our Committee did not see eye to eye with this suggestion and the Japanese never could understand it.

Sex brought other problems. It was difficult enough to take care of the people we had under such conditions as internment without having the additional responsibilities of increasing numbers of children on our hands. There was one young woman I remembered from Shanghai. She was caught by the war in Manila. She was forever falling in love, and by the end of the first year she had given birth, father unknown.

Once out of maternity, cupid stopped her again and at the end of the second year she had her second child. She was talked to seriously and firmly by both the authorities and the ecclesiastical representatives in our camp. Besides its being morally wrong, it was pointed out that we were running out of food and any children brought into the world at this point could not be properly cared for. But despite this, at the beginning of the third year she was noticed romancing nightly in the hall of the main building after lights-out and, of course, before liberation she had her third child.

What happened to the children? Your guess is as good as

mine. But you can rest assured that somebody among our well organized medical department, in cooperation with our internal charity organizations, saw to it that they were taken care of to the fullest extent of our resources, meager as they were.

Among all those people in Santo Tomas, there were bound to be some professional gamblers. It wasn't long after internment that they were playing their games wherever they could set them up. After lights-out at nine o'clock one group moved their table to the second floor of the Education Building, into my twelve-seater. It was the only spot where the lights were on all night and the talking and rattling of chips could not be heard.

Sometimes the game would carry on until morning when I showed up with my rubber hose and mop. This is when my authority meant something. My appearance meant, "move!"

You didn't have to be a gambler, however, to earn a peso at Santo Tomas. There were many who thought up various legal ways to increase the size of their pocketbooks. Among the entrepreneurs were Pop Caine and Brad Bradley. Pop was the number one garbage collector in the camp; and Bradley was an amateur chemist of sorts. When Pop collected the garbage, whenever we had any, he would pick out any bit of soap that anybody was fool enough to let slip through their fingers, then he and Brad, after forming it into bars, either sold or traded it.

This was profitable, but Bradley was the ambitious type and he could see a big market in the camp for ladies' shampoo. He searched for perfume and finally found a small bottle in the possession of Mrs. Russell Cannon, who, after some negotiation, sold it to him. Brad was able to squeeze three bottles of shampoo out of the perfume and left-over soap and sold them at fifteen pesos per bottle.

This was financially profitable, but the camp police put Mr. Bradley under arrest. The three women who had bought this wonder shampoo had lost their hair and looked like cue balls. Brad's defense was, "Can I help it, if I made it too strong?"

29

NEARLY EVERYONE HAS heard about the horrible tortures that the Japanese imposed on their prisoners. They have been noted for this throughout their history. It was first brought home to me in China, years before when Chiang Kai-shek's men were so brutally treated by the Nipponese in Manchuria in 1931. Friends of mine would bring these tales to me, but I was never really impressed with what the Japanese could do until one day at Santo Tomas when I saw a wheelbarrow being pushed through the entrance with what once had been the body of a man. There was still life, but that was about all. No one could recognize who it was.

A few days later, I visited our camp hospital and when I walked past a bed this, bleached-out bag of skin and bones motioned feebly with his hand for me to come closer.

"Don't you recognize me?" he whispered. His voice was barely audible. He indicated his passport which was by his bed. When I looked at it I was appalled to realize that the man lying in front of me was an old friend of mine from Shanghai by the name of Emuel Hammervich.

This was the story I pieced together. During the occupation of Manila the Japanese picked him up, but he convinced them that he was stateless, since he had just arrived from Shanghai. They permitted him his freedom and right away Emuel being a good businessman established a buy and sell company.

He did almost too well from the very beginning and

accumulated millions of Japanese pesos.

One day when Mr. Hammervich went to Baguio to close some kind of deal concerning trucks, the Japanese searched his room and found his American passport. Upon his return to Manila he was immediately arrested and from the very beginning underwent constant beating. When he was overcome by unconsciousness they threw him in a cell until he came to and then he was beat again. The next thing was the water cure, one version of which entails filling the body to capacity with water forced in by hose through openings other than the mouth.

They progressed with new tortures from there and experimented for future reference. Emuel Hammervich was practically dead after what he had been through and the Japs threw him in a cell ignoring him completely for a year giving him enough just food and water to prevent his death. During this time, he was in the prison of horrors at Fort Santiago.

When the Japanese were convinced he was going to die they dragged him into the street and laid his broken body, complete with passport, in the gutter. A Jap guard hailed a passing Filipino pushing a wheelbarrow and ordered, "Santo Tomas!" They wanted all the internees to see first hand what happened when you tried to fool the Japanese Army. Emuel Hammervich lived through it and saw the liberation by American troops.

The Japanese were terribly sensitive about their Emperor. Any implied insult was a major crime. Ponder for a moment the things in your daily life that you take for granted. Your morning cup of coffee, or tea, your automobile, your toothbrush, running water and your bathroom. During internment, we at Santo Tomas fared fairly well with my two twelve seaters and the other latrines throughout the camp and our supply committee saw to it as best they could that they were always clean and well supplied.

At Camp Holms, however, in Baguio, the summer capital of

I DIDN'T MAKE A MILLION

the Philippines, the internees in 1944 suffered an acute shortage of toilet paper. There was a considerable amount of agitation and finally the Japanese brought a truck load of unsold occupation newspapers up the two hundred miles from Manila.

On arrival a call was sent out over the loud speaker for volunteers to unload the truck and convey the bundles into a small warehouse. The whole camp showed up, but only twelve were chosen. After they had unloaded the newspapers they were ushered inside and placed around a large table. Then they were instructed to inspect each page of each newspaper and cut out any pictures of the Japanese Emperor. And to make sure no one overlooked the emperor on any of these pages, a Japanese guard stood behind each internee with a bayonet.

By 1943 Santo Tomas was so crowded that the Japanese opened another internment camp in Los Banos. A list was issued of able-bodied men to be transferred to the new site to build a camp. I volunteered to go but I was told that some able-bodied men would have to stay behind to carry out the details at Santo Tomas. I was quite proud of that – able-bodied, indeed! Shortly thereafter eight hundred men left for Los Banos in cattle cars; and as they left camp the loud speaker blasted away this song: Where Do We Go From Here Boys? Where Do We Go From Here?

Six months later, the boys had the camp in good enough condition so that their wives could join them. The Japs brought in twelve trucks to wheel the wives the eighty miles to their lonely husbands. Somebody with a sense of humor played over the loud speaking system the record, There'll Be a Hot Time In The Old Town Tonight.

Several times I have mentioned the loud speaker system and the records. This made running the camp much easier for the committee and the music was good for our morale. A very fine chap by the name of Don Bell ran the entertainment over the loud speaker and cheered up many a depressed soul with his programs. He used it for other purposes too. For example on the nineteenth of October 1944, our troops landed in Leyte. We knew about it through our hidden radios. The whole camp was so excited we could hardly contain ourselves. Don stuck his neck way out on a chopping block when he announced over the loud speaker system, "Attention, Mothers, Attention, Mothers. Tomorrow morning you may bring your children to the dental clinic at nine o'clock to have their teeth examined. You know, mothers, it is better Leyte than never."

It was like an electric shock. We almost forgot hunger that night. After the announcement disc jockey Bell played the record, Happy Days Are Here Again.

This was during the starvation period at Santo Tomas. The internees, especially the older ones, were dying off rapidly. Every night the little native horse was heard cloppity-clopping through the camp, drawing its carretela with a mysterious box aboard. We knew as he passed that someone else had been "liberated" – by hunger.

We had eaten virtually everything there was to eat inside the camp and the people outside were starving as well. Our daily ration from the Japanese was one handful of rice plus whatever our Committee could dig up for us. Together there was far from enough.

At the beginning there had been hundreds and hundreds of imported pigeons nesting in the belfries of the main building and chapel. I can remember the evenings and early mornings when the pigeons came down in the yard and we would feed them bread and rice. But as the food was cut down we had less and less pigeons. One morning, at five o'clock, I saw Dave Darcie standing behind a tree holding a long pole with a net on the end of it. As I watched him: smoosh! Four or five pigeons were scooped up and Dave was running like heck for his shanty.

In 1943 Helen and I had found a little black kitten playing in the camp and decided to take it to our shanty as a pet. It was a cute little cat and gave us many hours of amused enjoyment. In 1944, however, when things got tough, both Helen and I began to eye that cat as the hungry days passed. But somehow, we just could not bring ourselves to it. One night, Blackie failed to show up and Helen was worried. I went out between the shanties and hollered to the extent of my strength, "Kitty, kitty! Here, Blackie. Kitty, kitty, kitty." But nothing happened. We went to bed hungry and forgot about the cat until the next morning when I was going to my labor detail. I walked past a garbage can, the sole contents of which was one black at skin. My neighbor, an Englishman, had had a cat banquet, inviting his friends to dine.

Helen and I had not eaten any cats, but we got so hungry that one rainy night we decided to test the veracity of a current camp rumor that the roots of banana trees were edible. We waited until after midnight and then like a couple of second story men we left our shanty and trekked through the mud toward a banana tree that we had been watching for days. We stalked this tree like a tabby cat does a robin and when we arrived safely at its base, we took turns digging around it. After an hour of labor, expending energy we couldn't afford, we dragged the roots back to our shanty. Helen put on the water to boil and we cleaned the root as best we could, cutting it up in chunks.

I just couldn't wait for that banana root to get cooked! Helen kept testing it and then let it boil some more. Finally, when she dished out two plates full we made the earth-shaking discovery that banana roots have no food value. The next day, however, Helen diced the chunks and toasted them. We ate what we could, at least to have something in our stomachs.

In the early days when we had actual bananas somebody

WHITEY SMITH

dropped a banana skin on the floor on the second story of the Education Building. When I saw it I picked it up and threw it in the waste basket. This was a simple act but it earned me a great deal of publicity because Mr. Theo Rogers, general manager of the *Philippines Free Press* for want of something better to do had been watching that banana peel for some considerable time to see how long it would be before somebody picked up the dangerous thing-or slipped on it and busted his neck.

To appreciate the humor of this fully it is necessary to know Theo Rogers. He is famous in the Philippines for a short gray beard and for the fact, he will expound at great length on any subject at all with the minimum of encouragement.

The day I picked up the banana peel it was but a matter of minutes before Mr. Rogers had a crowd gathered in the hall where he put his arm around me talking about the virtuous Whitey Smith and how everybody else was a slacker compared to a man like Whitey Smith, who would stoop to picking up a banana peel. The thing about it is, besides being a latrine cleaner, I was the hall cleaner too, and I was supposed to pick things up!

30

I HAD CLEANED toilets and hallways for two and a half years and had worn out all my shoes and boots and even my wooden *bakyas*. I slushed around in my bare feet for some weeks and finally took the tops of my shoes to the sanitation committee and asked that they be resoled. They acted as if they didn't know where I worked after having made me latrine supervisor a mere two and a half years ago. When I refreshed their memory they turned me down flat, saying that they fixed shoes for those who worked in sanitation outdoors only.

This didn't set too well and I told them, "I quit. Get somebody else to clean your toilets," and my hundred and ten pounds and I took a vacation.

It wasn't long before my name was called over the loud speaker instructing me to report to the labor department. Before they even had a chance to say anything to me I told them defiantly that I refused to clean any more toilets. I would do anything else, but no more commode duty.

I was really surprised when they asked me if I was willing to work on the rice cleaning machine. I jumped at the chance. Rice meant food. But I found out that the rice I cleaned each day went out of the camp; and besides that, there was a Japanese guard there who had absolutely no ambition in life other than to watch my every move to prevent me from taking even one ittbitty grain of rice.

Helen scrounged some cloth and made two long extra pockets

which hung between my legs. They would hold quite a lot of rice. Every now and then Helen and I had a meal and once in a while, if I had a good day, we invited in the neighbors.

Apparently I was not the only rice cleaner who had sticky fingers. I was the only worker in the mill who lived across the camp, and when the air raid signal was on I couldn't get to work. On one of my absent days the Japs made a raid and found rice in every worker's pocket. They sent all but me to the camp prison until liberation.

With my rice racket working Helen and I were enjoying an extra meal one day when my dental bridge went boom and there I was with four teeth missing right in front. As far as eating went I didn't have to worry much, but oh my vanity! I looked like heck. Next morning, I went over to see our American dentist, Doc Fanton, and he shook his head and said I was out of luck. The Japs had barred all Filipino doctors and dentists and he had no extra teeth.

That night Doc came to my bunk after lights-out and said he had made a contact over the fence. Get two hundred pesos he said and come over to the office tomorrow so I can make an impression. I waited three weeks and the teeth arrived. The "outside" had stuck some different sized teeth into a contraption that Doc said was made of gutta percha. When he pushed that handful of teeth into my mush I looked like the original horse's mouth. When I looked into a mirror I could have done a Jekyll and Hyde. I still have the teeth but I don't wear them. I'm holding them for a spare. There maybe another war.

Besides food being in short supply, fuel was also on the critical list. Fortunately the tropical warmth made heating unnecessary, but when we did pick up something to eat it usually needed to be cooked. We had even chopped and burned the miserable steps to our shanty and every other extra piece of wood that we could find. Phil Crovat, a neighbor of mine who was just able to move his six-foot four-inch hundred and ten pound body around, had had his eye on the school benches scattered here and there throughout the campus.

Phil woke me up one night and said, "Whitey, the Japs will never miss one of those school benches." And I agreed. So we made our way to the nearest one and, crawling on our hands and knees, brought it back to our area. We would push and pull it about a foot at a time until we got it to the road and then we carried it as fast as we could in our condition to our shanty. Then out came the ax and hocus pocus! A stack of firewood!

We took only one bench at a time, of course, and only when we had to have it, but even so the Japs noticed that their seating arrangement wasn't what it used to be. They began searching the shanties for their benches and when they couldn't find them they got kind of crabby about it. Fortunately the Japs never got as far as Helen's and my shanty and by the time of liberation most of them were sitting on the ground.

Some of the internees with a sense of humor took the hunger that we all hated so much and used it as a vehicle for practical jokes. There were two pre-war millionaires in our camp who palled around together and who were not averse to pulling jokes on each other. They were Mr. Henry Belden and Mr. Amos Bellis.

Both were anxious to be of help in the camp and they did the best they could. Henry worked in the hospital from twelve midnight until six each morning. One of the gates to the hospital was guarded by Amos who came on duty at six in the morning and worked until noon. One morning, Henry came off duty with a toothpick in his mouth, wiping off his chin with his handkerchief as if he had just eaten.

Amos who had just come on duty noticed this and asked Henry, as he had a hundred times before, how his job was.

Incidentally, did he get anything extra to eat? Henry looked around as if to make sure that no one was listening and then told Amos to keep it quiet, that he had just had bacon and eggs with two cups of coffee. Henry winked and walked away rubbing his stomach and juggling the toothpick from side to side in his mouth.

Needless to say, this impressed Amos Bellis. He couldn't wait for Henry to get out of sight and to get someone to spell him at the gate while he went over to the labor office to apply for an assignment in the hospital. At the time of liberation Amos Bellis was still on the waiting list. You should hear those two laugh about that today!

Lack of food affected the women, too, but I can never understand the method some of them used to try to forget their hunger. Many of them would sit in circles of an evening during the starvation period and with paper and pencil at hand, if they could find such items, swap recipes. I had to walk away when these sessions started. I couldn't be hungrier than I was, but the mere thought of food almost put me in a state of shock.

Some of the men were just as bad on this score. One evening a group of us stood in the second floor hallway of the Education Building discussing anything but food. Up walked an old gentleman, a mining engineer, and began to tell the story about the time he was in Baltimore and saw in a bakery window a great big cherry pie with an inch thick crust and cherry juice seeping through in big sweet drops. He told how he went inside, bought the pie, ate three quarters of it, and threw the rest away.

He was lucky to get away from us alive. We hardly spoke to him for the rest of the internment because every time we saw him we thought of that cherry pie – not the part he ate but the part he threw away.

Despite our intense hunger the great majority of the internees did not lose their responsibility toward their fellow man. If any of us got food we tried to share it with as many as we could. One evening after my labor detail I dragged myself to our shanty and just made the door before I fell down. I was certain that if I didn't get some food soon I was going to die. I managed to pull myself inside and into my bunk, and prayed for strength. As I lay there wondering what was going to happen to all of us I heard a whisper.

"Whitey, bring a plate. Whitey, bring a plate."

Even if it were my imagination I thought I'd take a chance so I staggered out of my bunk, picked up a plate and made my way outside. Peeking around the corner of my shanty was Mrs. Dodge, my next door neighbor, motioning for me to join her. When I got to her window she surreptitiously handed me a bone.

"Here," she said, "Give this to Helen to boil. It will make good soup. I got the meat."

I had a new lease on life. Helen boiled that bone and I have never tasted such absolutely magnificent beef bouillon. When Helen and I had drunk our fill, I took what was left to Phil Crovat's shanty. He was flat on his back. I lifted his head and poured some soup down him and he whispered, "Whitey, you have saved my life, you have saved my life. " I told him not to worry because we would boil the bone again.

To me, this was like bread on the water. A month before I had put my hands on a dozen eggs and I had given Mrs. Dodge six.

Some people suffered almost as much from the lack of tobacco as they did from the lack of food. Whenever you were lucky enough to get a cigarette or cigar it was smoked a few puffs at a time, extinguished and then lit again later. When the butt burned your lips the little bit that remained was carefully hoarded and when enough was accumulated you would search out a piece of toilet tissue and roll one.

WHITEY SMITH

There was one man in camp who seemed never to run out of cigars. He was Tommy Jordan, a prominent insurance executive in Manila, and even up to liberation he had cigars. For months he had been down to one a day but I used to follow him around to get the butt and take it home, chop it up, dry it carefully over the charcoal burner and then roll one.

I knew that Tommy must have a supply of these Coronas hidden somewhere. Since I couldn't find them, I thought I'd try a little psychology. I went to his bunk one day and started a conversation, picking a time when he was down in the dumps and blue. His wife and daughter were in the U.S.A. and he sometimes doubted if he would ever see them again. On this day, I told him that I had just heard some good news but to keep it to himself. Uncle Sam, I said, had brought a thousand planes into Burma to use against the Japs and we had landed troops somewhere in the southern Philippines. He was ecstatic. Making sure no one was looking, he reached somewhere in his bunk and pulled out a cigar and said, "Whitey, that's the best news I've heard in two and a half years. Have a cigar." That smoke lasted me a week.

One of the happiest days of my life was on the third of February, 1945, when a tank burst through the gate of Santo Tomas. At first we didn't know whether it was Japanese or American but as it got closer to our side of camp we heard the internees singing, "God Bless America," and we knew we were free. We were hysterical and crying with happiness.

The Japanese had barricaded themselves in the Education Building with two hundred and fifty of our internees who were later freed when the Jap guards were marched out of camp under escort. In their hurry the Japanese left their trucks out in front of the building full of luggage. I told Helen to follow me and, while the excitement and shooting was going on we sneaked up to one

I DIDN'T MAKE A MILLION

of the trucks and in the back we found many canvas knapsacks. There was one blue one which I figured belonged to an officer so I took it and Helen and I dragged it into our shanty.

Inside we found five kilos of rice, forty-two packages of cigarettes, a big bag of sugar, and, among other things, a big jar of Heinz pickles. Helen made a fire and while everybody else was milling around I got some of our hungry neighbors and we had a feast. I passed the cigarettes keeping a few packages for ourselves and then Helen and I fell into an exhausted sleep.

The next morning the GI's had set up chow for everybody and the loud speaker announced "Come and get it, bring your own bucket." Helen and I started to do just that, but on the way over , the tank's fifty-caliber machine gun went off. The bullet went right between my legs and hit the granite wall of the main building. The concussion knocked me out and when I came to I had a nick in my leg. A piece of granite had flown back and hit me just below the knee. I fell in the gutter with blood streaming down my leg.

It seems that a GI was cleaning his machine gun, but he forgot to take the round out of the chamber. So after three years in that place, what happens the day I'm freed? My first meal of good solid American food, which I had been waiting for so long, was postponed by a piece of granite from the very walls that had imprisoned me.

31

IT WAS THE last of March 1945 when Helen and I walked away from Santo Tomas. Helen was in bad shape but still she had stood it better than I. I weighed one hundred four pounds and since I am almost six feet tall, I looked pretty gruesome. I was forty-eight years old, but I looked seventy.

It was so wonderful to be free again, but we had no money and no place to go. We had pesos in the National City Bank of New York but that was still closed. I had friends though, and the United States Armed Forces. Those guys wouldn't let you starve.

Everybody was scrambling to get back into their old way of life again, trying to forget the internment. Many had died in camp and many were still in the hospital and still more remained in their shanties, either because they were not prewar residents of the Philippines or in any case had absolutely nothing to go to outside, no homes, no business.

For a full month after liberation the Japanese had kept the internment camp under shellfire. General MacArthur paid us a visit one day and announced afterward that the city of Manila had fallen to the American forces. That to us seemed a slight exaggeration. The worst of the fighting came after that and it resulted in complete destruction of about twothirds of the city. Upwards of forty of our internees were killed by exploding shells right inside the camp. It was a horrible time, but we were all so happy over being liberated that we weren't as scared or as cautious as we should have been and we suffered for it. A few who slipped outside during those times were brought back in baskets and some never got back at all.

The saddest story was what happened to our committee chairman, Carroll Grinnell, and three other fine fellows who had been instrumental in running the camp and protecting us as much as they could from the Japanese. The other three were A. F. Duggleby, a mining man of exceptional character and ability; E. E. Johnson, a prominent American businessman who had been caught by the war in Manila, and C. L. Larsen, the unluckiest one of all.

On Christmas eve of 1944 the Japanese "picked up" all four men. Orders from Fort Santiago. I think they caught Grinnell in his office, where he spent most of his time. The others they found in their shanties or rooms. They were taken out of camp into the city under guard, very quietly. A pall fell over the camp on Christmas day. We knew something awful was up, but we didn't know what.

Piece by piece the story came out. We didn't learn all of it until after liberation. They were accused of having guerrilla contacts and of sending information, money and assistance to Americans in prison camps up in Tarlac province and Nueva Ecija. They were tortured, mutilated and finally beheaded. Their bodies were found by our American intelligence people and buried with honors in a little plot in the hospital compound just outside the walls of the internment camp. They were all decorated posthumously by our government.

Poor Larsen. He was as meek and quiet and inoffensive as anyone could be. He didn't know any guerrillas and never stuck his neck out. He was a plain good citizen, in or out of prison and the only thing wrong with him was that his name was Larsen. The Japanese were looking for another Larsen, an executive of the Standard Oil Company with the same or very similar initials.

It was a plain case of mistaken identity. The rest were all guilty as charged. To us they were heroes; to the Japanese, criminals.

Those of us who had been in Manila before the war anticipated that now Uncle Sam was moving in again there would be a boom in business. People needed so many things and all the GI's had to be entertained, thousands and thousands of them. That's where Helen and I figured we came in. We wanted to get back into the night club business and the first thing we needed was money.

As I mentioned earlier, Helen and I had buried twenty thousand pesos' worth of diamonds on a mountainside near Los Banos before we surrendered to the Japanese. We were sure that if somebody hadn't found them by now that with the intense growth of Philippine vegetation we could never find the place we buried our jewels anyhow. Nonetheless, it was in the back of my mind and one day I asked two GI friends of mine, Sergeant Oscar and Private Sack, if they would help me find our buried fortune. They would. Without saying a word to Helen (because there were Japs around and they weren't housebroken) the three of us took off early one morning for Los Banos and Mt. Makiling.

Halfway there we met a lieutenant, who was in charge of a nearby GI-run saw mill providing much needed lumber for the Army. I told him where we were going and he told me it was dangerous because there were still Jap patrols in the area. Just yesterday, he said, they had met and killed five Japanese soldiers, and he was sure there were many more around. He said the five bodies were just up the road.

I thought it over. After three years in internment it would be hell to get shot after I was free. My two GI friends agreed that they would go along, so I said OK.

The lieutenant called four Filipino guerrillas to guide me, handed me a Garand rifle and hung fifty rounds of ammunition around my neck. My one hundred and four pounds had a real struggle under that load. The rifle felt like a cannon. The lieutenant was encouraging when he said if they heard any shooting they would come right away.

Sure enough, just as the lieutenant had said, not far up the road were the bodies of five Japanese. A few miles beyond that the Filipino guerrillas refused to go any further because they felt sure there were too many Japs ahead for safety. We drove as far as we could and then traveled up a dry river bed on foot over boulders and stones. I was soaking wet and nearly exhausted when we arrived at what I thought was the place we had buried our diamonds. As I expected, three years had changed everything and I couldn't get my bearings. We turned back sadly.

We returned to the sawmill to give the lieutenant back his rifle and ammunition and I passed out in a dead faint. The medics gave me some first aid and then Oscar, Sack and I returned to Manila.

Helen was put out with me. She had a hunch where I had gone and wanted to be included in the search. Some thirty days later, Helen tried her luck at finding our buried valuables, but like me she was not successful. I told her to forget it. The bank would open soon and we'd have some money to start on.

After liberation, I had gone to inspect my old place, the Metro Garden and Grill. All that was left were the tables and chairs. For many reasons, I couldn't reopen the Metro, so at the request of the 11th Airborne, I let them take my tables and chairs to use in their officer's club. Now that I was trying to open a new night club this favor came in handy. The 11th Airborne pulled out to take part in the proposed invasion of Japan and when they left they returned my tables and chairs and all the extra materials that they had. This meant that I had paint, pipe, lumber, masonite, electric wires, switches and bulbs. But I had no place to put them.

In desperation, I went to an old Spanish friend who lived just across the street from Santo Tomas. Right away he took me to a big two-story building, not far from Malacanang Palace. Even though it was half shot to pieces it would still do. But there was a big sign on the front that said "U.S. Army Property, Keep Out", and my spirits fell. My Spanish friend took me to the owner and since the army was not actually using the building, he said I could have a two-year lease at seven hundred pesos per month, three months in advance.

We signed the papers and I gave him a post-dated check for the balance. Helen and I went to visit our new found nightclub site and discovered some army captain had just moved three hundred sixty-five refugees into the building. I protested vehemently but I was afraid to push it too far, since my lease was kind of shaky. I agreed to "allow" the refugees to stay a couple of weeks until they could find a place for themselves. But the captain was transferred and I was afraid to call on any other authority to move these people out. So Helen and I moved in with them.

All this time Helen had our buried diamonds on her mind. After my failure and her disappointment, I was convinced it was no use. But Helen was not going to let twenty thousand pesos slip through her fingers that easily when we needed the money so badly. She took some of our friends with her and somehow located our last camp on the mountainside. All of them began to dig over a large area. No diamonds.

They were just about to leave when Helen took her eyes off the ground and found herself looking at a large stone propped in the lower branches of a bamboo tree. It looked familiar. She walked over closer and became excited. She recognized it and reasoned that while she had planted it on the ground the bamboo had grown up around it and lifted it with growth. She looked upward and there, about thirty feet high, were three notches which she had cut in a baby bamboo sprout a yard tall.

They dug up the tree and under it found the ashes from our last camp fire that Helen had thrown into our treasure hole. She got down on her hands and knees and dug like a puppy dog. Finally, she squealed with joy and with a little more digging came up with our can of diamonds. Just like a fairy tale. I think that is when our luck began to turn.

I had made a loose agreement with four internment and prewar pals to go in with me on a night club. They were all as busted as I was and one of them was still in a prison camp in Japan. They were interested in setting up a gambling room on the side if I could get a club going.

Soon after our diamond recovery, one of the "Big Four" drove up with a big truck load of sugar sacks that he had obtained through a barter deal for lumber. I didn't know what we were going to do with sugar sacks but I stored them. A few days later I took one of the sacks with me and headed by jeepney for someplace, I can't recall at the present.

The man sitting next to me fingered the sack and said he would like to buy some if I had any extra to sell. He wanted them for the drapes in his office. I obliged him with seventy sacks at five pesos each. Not long after that a gentleman came and bought a thousand to use in his Ideal Theater for stage curtains. This was five thousand pesos more. Another man from the Avenue Theater came to buy some more sacks which I sold for six pesos apiece and added six thousand pesos more to our balance.

In desperation I moved all the refugees to the bottom floor and with the material I had received from the 11th Airborne Officers Club and what else I could buy we began to fix up the top floor as a night club. We had laughingly referred to this building as our "mansion" and it followed logically then that we decided to call our club the "Old Mansion."

WHITEY SMITH

Helen took the remaining sugar sacks and draped them all over our new nightclub. We had drapes behind the bar, on the walls, and we used the sacks also as table cloths and runners. Slowly we were getting into business. But there was a lot of hard work remaining.

32

WE HAD MOST everything we needed now to open up the Old Mansion except liquor, dishes and glasses. The dishes could come later when we could get food to serve, but the glasses we had to have right away. Helen's ingenuity solved that. I got six hundred empty beer bottles from the army and Helen took them one by one and made glasses out of them simply by placing a red hot wire around the bottle just below the neck and immersing it quickly into cold water. Pop! the bottle snapped in two where the wire was. After she had applied emery cloth – scrounged from the army – to the sharp rims and made them smooth enough to use with safety, we had glasses.

All I had to worry about now was the liquor and ice. I had hired a band and there was plenty of help available and my clientele was almost built-in providing I had something to serve. The distilling industry in the Philippines like everything else had been hurt by the Japanese occupation. The most prominent distillery was owned and operated, and still is, by the Elizalde family. (One of the Elizalde brothers was executed for his pro-allied activities).

There wasn't much of a supply of spirits when the war was over and even though the distilleries began running full blast after liberation they still couldn't satisfy the demand.

I went to the Elizalde Company office to buy what I needed but found a line, mostly GI's, two blocks long ahead of me. I made my way through another path to the office and they agreed to give me eighteen hundred pesos' worth of locally made Scotch, rum, and gin. The Scotch, called "Old Special," was sixty-five proof, just a few weeks old and cost sixteen pesos per bottle. I agreed to pay for it within forty-eight hours. We opened the Old Mansion the next day.

The army helped with our ice requirement, although it wasn't exactly under official circumstances. The army ice plant was just next door to me. I had obtained permission from Colonel Andres Soriano, who was then serving in the military, to get three hundred pounds for my opening night, but that was all. On the open market, ice cost one hundred pesos or fifty dollars for a three-hundred pound block and it wasn't exactly safe to use, either.

On a hunch, I went to see the sergeant in charge of the ice plant. I told him there would be a table all set for the sergeant and his WAC girl friends at my place every night and I was just next door.

"Whitey," said the sergeant with a grin, "You've got all the ice you need."

For a soup plate of ice in the Old Mansion we received four pesos, while a drink cost three. When a customer got his check it would read something like: ice, forty-six pesos; drinks, forty pesos. But nobody complained and we always had a full house.

Uncle Sam helped me get electricity, too. The Manila Electric Company was in very limited operation, straining to generate the power to provide people with necessities – and night clubs in anybody's language are not classed under the heading of necessities. But with me it was now or never and I had to figure out some way to light the Old Mansion's many light bulbs.

Right next door to the club was a unit of the Counter Intelligence Corps, called the CIC for short. Behind it ran the Pasig River. The CIC had its power generator right on the river shore. I'm glad they did. Among my employees was a Filipino I had known for years and was aware that he had one time tried out for a swimming team to represent his province or college at a swimming meet. I asked him if he could swim in the Pasig River and he said yes. I gave him a wire and told him I would meet him at a designated spot downstream. He jumped in the water and I hurried next door and met my aquatic employee near the large CIC generator. In exchange for a season ticket to the Old Mansion, the generator night watchman let me plug in and we had lights. When we closed my employee swam back again, disconnected the wire and returned with it. This went on for months until the Manila Electric Company could provide full power.

A couple of times the army became suspicious about how I got my lights, but every time they inspected my place I would show them a one-lung generator I had picked up second hand. It couldn't have furnished enough electricity to light ten bulbs, but I kept it put-putting away for effect.

The Old Mansion did very well from the first night on. We had our trials and tribulations, but we made money. The Big Four were operating successfully on the premises, and although I didn't know it at the time, they formed a closed syndicate to control gambling in the entire city of Manila. They all had operated in the city before the war and their idea was to have the gambling proceeds go into one pot with nobody running competition. I was not included in this organization but I went ahead and built living quarters at the Old Mansion for the four of them. I could see trouble coming.

About this time a lieutenant in the army who had been a regular customer, approached me and asked if I could use a few chickens for the holidays. "Why yes, thanks," I said, I thought he meant for Christmas for Helen and me. We could buy chicken on the open market but they were not the Stateside type.

Next morning at four o'clock one of the servants told me that an officer was down in the yard and wanted to see me right away. I put on a bathrobe and went down. First thing I thought was that somebody had found out about my wire into the CIC generator, but downstairs in the front yard I found a six-by-six truck loaded with cases of cold storage chickens.

My first reaction was absolute panic. All I needed now was a truck-load of government chickens and I would spend three more years in prison.

"For God's sake, get those things out of here!" I almost screamed. The lieutenant looked hurt but he jumped into the truck and the driver backed out of our driveway. I was in a cold sweat. In the middle of my third sigh of relief the lieutenant, truck and eighty-four cases of cold storage chickens were back at my gate. I tried to ignore them but one peep out of that GI horn which sounded like the loudest thing in the world and I practically tore that gate down with my bare hands.

The lieutenant was excited and very nervous, second only to me. "Whitey, here are your chickens." I could have killed him.

"But I don't want that many chickens!" I protested.

"But I have no where else to deliver the load!" he countered. And with that, men who had been in the back of the truck somewhere began unloading.

I dashed back and forth in my bathrobe saying, "no, no, no"! and the lieutenant jumped back and forth between the truck and the street as if he expected General MacArthur along any minute.

The moment that truck was empty it pulled out and there I stood. What I had was eighty-four cases of "hot" chicken, which (a) belonged to somebody else, and (b) that somebody else was Uncle Sam and if there is anybody in the world whose property you do not want to have in your hands without his knowing about it, it's Uncle Sam.

I pulled myself together enough to know I had to do something. I stacked the chickens in my garage and covered them with old newspapers. Then I went upstairs and crawled back into bed. All I could see was chickens! I was shaking so hard I almost shook apart and I lay awake until the break of day.

When I asked my cook how many chickens he could use he said about eight. Then I called all my employees together and stacked their arms full. Within a couple of hours people were clamoring at my gate. They all knew I was giving away chickens. With this I suffered another in a long series of panics. The only thing I could think of was to throw the chickens out of my back window into the Pasig River and that's exactly what I did! I kept four cases for our own use and then had them for breakfast, lunch and dinner and in between meals, too!

A few days later the lieutenant came back to the Old Mansion and said to me, "Whitey, how about some hams?" I said, "Lieutenant, don't ever do such a thing to me again." And with that I escorted him to the door, although I appreciated his apparently good intentions and said emphatically, "You shall not return."

33

AFTER THE CHICKEN crisis had passed, things went along smoothly except for the impression I received from the Big Four that I wasn't a part of the Old Mansion. We were building a gaming room upstairs and it really looked good. One early morning, a friend of one of the Big Four, a great big guy, showed up. He was about the size of Primo Carnera, and went by the name of Izzy. He was supposed to be a big-shot importer. Izzy moved in, bag and baggage. He was big not only in size but in talk, and within a week he acted like he was the boss and I was the janitor. I definitely had the feeling I was being muscled out.

Izzy right away began taking orders for liquor and cigarettes which were supposed to be coming from the States. The local Chinese buyers were giving him deposits which were guaranteed by the Big Four. This business got so good that Izzy opened an office downstairs in the club.

The next thing I knew Izzy said that he had won the bid on two hundred thousand cases of beer at Clark Air Force Base, fifty miles north of Manila. They had a lawyer draw up the necessary forms to establish an import and export corporation and we all met together for lunch one day to sign our names. The lawyer started the document around the table but when it got to me, whish! it went right by my nose. This was embarrassing and I was miffed. I got up and asked, "Has everybody signed? If so, I hope you all make a million." Then I went out into the bar.

While I was there one of the Big Four came out to me and

I DIDN'T MAKE A MILLION

said, "Say, Whitey, you should insure the club."

Well, what do you know. I found the building, I built the club, I got the license, I got the electricity, I got the glasses, and I arranged living quarters for the Big Four, and the club was entertaining their friends nightly, and now I should insure it for them!

Later the big four had a meeting and they "sent" for me. They wanted to know why I had a right to anything in their corporation or gambling concession. I told them exactly how I felt and after all my work and since it was virtually my business I thought I had a right to have a share. They informed me, however, that I had never had anything to start with and that I would be adequately taken care of working out in front and that was all I was entitled to. I had been muscled out!

On the way downstairs I met Izzy and made a quick decision. I told Izzy that I was tired after my three years internment and wanted to quit the business. I offered him my "share" for fifty thousand pesos.

"Izzy," I said, "if l were you I wouldn't say anything about my offer to the other fellows. Why don't you think it over and let me know?"

Izzy couldn't wait to get up those stairs and pass the word. Soon I was "sent for" again. Oh, they said, so you think we can't get along without you, huh? Think, we can't run this joint without Whitey Smith, huh? What makes you think your share is worth fifty thousand pesos, huh? I told them that I had built the club and said that all they needed was complete control and they would make a million. Out of a clear blue sky Izzy said it was a deal and gave me a check. The Big Four tried to talk me out of it but I was on my way to the bank. Izzy's liquor and cigarettes never came in and Ted had to make good the deposit because after he paid me fifty thousand pesos he had just about enough money left to buy one bottle of beer.

To top it off the two hundred thousand cases of beer that the corporation was supposed to have at Clark Field, they were informed, really belonged to the Navy at Cavite. So Whitey Smith had fifty thousand pesos and the Big Four had sacks.

A few nights later I went out to visit the El Cairo Club in Quezon City which was five miles from Manila. It was a great big place built of bamboo, sawali and rattan, capable of holding at least six hundred people. It was run by two partners, Johnny Ismael and Solo Garcia. When I arrived George Rowe, a decorated guerrilla commander, invited me to sit at his table and the party began. Johnny Ismael was sitting at our table enjoying the fun.

After a while, for a joke, George Rowe said to Johnny, "What do you have to do around this joint to get a drink? Your service is terrible."

Johnny laughed and said, "If you think it's so bad why don't you buy the place?"

George Rowe looked at me and said in surprising seriousness, "Whitey, why don't we?" And we closed the deal right there. On the night of January 4, 1946, the Club El Cairo opened under our management.

Our place became a must to the night life crowd of Manila. It was boom time and there was plenty of money. We knew that within three years all the spots down town would be rehabilitated and draw our crowd away so we made hay while the moon shone. We built an air-conditioned cocktail lounge and did a roaring business.

A derby hat walked into El Cairo one night. Underneath it was a man wearing old-fashioned clothes and on his arm was a nice looking lady, middle aged I would say. The lady was his wife and the man under the derby was Joe Grove, my old Burma oil friend. The first thing we asked as we threw our arms around each other was, "Where's my watch?" He didn't have mine and I didn't have his. But it didn't make any difference now.

Joe was walking with a cane – like he really depended on it too. You never could tell when Joe was doing well or not doing so good because his clothes always looked like he was doing bad. But I could see there was something wrong. Mrs Grove acted as if she was expecting Joe to tell me something.

I kept asking Joe how things were. And according to him, things had never been better. Things were fine. How about the cane? I asked. Well, he had joined the British Army as a major when World War II started and had been shot in the leg. He was taking a cruise on a freighter now for his health. But, yeah, things were great.

Two and two began to make four. Before, Joe always traveled first class. Now he was traveling by freighter. He was superintendent of the Burma Oil Fields when I knew him last, a job for an active man, but now he walked with a cane. Besides that, the missus didn't look as if they were in the chips. Also she appeared to be in mental distress.

I excused myself and went into the gambling casino of my club and asked the manager if we had any U.S. dollars. We did. I brought a stack back to the table and put it in Joe's pocket. Joe was embarrassed and Mrs. Grove just sat and looked for almost a minute, then all of a sudden she stood up and shouted."The drinks are on me! The drinks are on me!"Then she sat down.

"Whitey," said Mrs. Grove, "This is the first time my husband has been right since I married him! He said if we find Whitey we will be all right. God bless you, Whitey."

Joe was on his way to the States to retire. I was right. He wasn't doing too well. God bless him. I heard he died a few years ago.

Helen and I had been out of internment now for over two years. The El Cairo Club was doing fine and we thought it time to take a vacation. It was 1947 and Helen and I decided to play the millionaire for sixty days, leaving the club in the capable hands of my manager, Jack Cohen.

We took twenty-five thousand American dollars, got aboard a luxury liner and went to the United States. The first thing I did, when we got off the ship, was buy a new Cadillac. This accomplished, we got new gowns, shoes and accessories for Helen and a new wardrobe for me. Then we started to enjoy ourselves.

I had found out in San Francisco that a couple of old buddies of mine were running a bar on Franklin Street in my old home town of Oakland. They called it The Ringside but most of Oakland knew it as the poor man's Stork Club.

Helen and I drove up in front of the Ringside in our big long Cadillac. We walked inside and there was Harold Broom, my old friend from years gone by frying fish behind the counter for a customer. The customer was Tom Ross, who, since I saw him last, had gone blind. I recognized him, of course, and grabbed his hand saying, "Do you know who I am?"

"I can't see you," he said, "But I know your voice. You're Whitey Smith." I almost cried, because I hadn't seen Tom Ross for years and years. He was a boyhood pal of mine. Harold Broom's partner was another old friend of mine, Jim Dundee, whom I had fought on three occasions when we were both kids. Jimmy, at one point, was Oakland's featherweight champ.

Harold and Jimmy were trying to raise money so that Tom Ross could have an operation on his eyes. Helen and I made our contribution, but even though it wasn't large they judged from our Cadillac and new clothes, and started a rumor. Whitey Smith had made a million dollars in the Far East! It felt so good I didn't deny it because I figured I could hang on as a millionaire for sixty days.

I DIDN'T MAKE A MILLION

I took Tom out and bought him a new suit of clothes, shoes and hat and what goes with it. Then I asked him if he would round up all my old boyhood friends and invite them to a party after the fights scheduled at the auditorium (I wouldn't miss those in Oakland) that night. I had rented the penthouse on top of the T and D Theater and loaded it.

We had ringside seats at the fights and I was introduced by Jimmy Murray, the boxing promoter of Oakland, as the local boy who made good. After the card was over we all went to my penthouse party and brought along a lot of people I hadn't counted on, but I was glad they came. We had fighters and politicians, including the vice-mayor and Gene Murphy, a retired detective hero. I had six cases of champagne left over so I asked Jimmy Dundee to telephone the captain of police and asked him to send his policemen to the Ringside as they got off duty to receive a take-home bottle of champagne with the compliments of a squarehead from Watts Track.

After that night I never could convince anybody in Oakland that I didn't make a million.

34

HELEN AND I MILLIONED our way up to Reno and stayed long enough to thin down our bankroll. Then we just traveled around until we got tired of it and went back to Oakland. We sold the car and returned to our second home, the Philippines. Our friends had cooked up a celebration. There were bands and banners and a lot of fun. El Cairo was going bigger and better than ever.

Rehabilitation of downtown Manila was coming along rapidly and we foresaw that soon our business would dwindle. We were too far from the center of things. New clubs were opening on Dewey Boulevard and the more accessible ones were sure to get the play. We voluntarily closed Club El Cairo while we were still ahead. It had been a lot of fun, it had enabled us to play the millionaire for sixty days and we had money in the bank.

We built a nice big house in Quezon City and Helen and I tried to retire. It wasn't easy. The nightclub business beckoned to us a couple of times and we tried it on our own, but the excitement and challenge had gone out of it. I was still looking for that million dollars, and in 1951 I was sure once more that I had it made. I was going to be the Fertilizer King of the Philippines.

It all began one morning when I was on my way down town. An old-timer I knew in Santo Tomas named George Parsons hailed me from the sidewalk and started talking.

George had a wife and three kids and since the liberation he had had a desperate time trying to make ends meet. He was kind of an amateur chemist along with other things and this had led him to a scheme which on this sunny morning he asked me to finance.

George was very persuasive and at the time his proposition sounded to me to be almost foolproof, if George knew what he was talking about. He called my attention to all the water hyacinths that floated down the Pasig River. They looked like waterlilies. Millions of them passed through Manila each day on their way to the sea. As a matter of fact, George said, there were so many that some of the smaller boats were having a hard time getting through. The old-timer told me that those lilies were a veritable gold mine because he was almost sure that they contained a certain required percentage of a certain something that would make high grade fertilizer. George talked in such glowing terms that if he had some of that certain percentage of whatever he was looking for in his possession I would have rubbed some on my balding head. I was sold.

Surreptitiously we lined up two trucks, keeping the whole thing secret, and went to a remote spot on the Pasig and began loading water lilies. The truck drivers thought we were crazy then; they thought we were utterly insane when we took the water lilies ten miles into the country and began cooking them. We cooked lilies for days. First we dried them in the sun and then placed them in two large oil drums which we had set up on cement blocks. George kept running his fingers through the cooked lilies, nodding his head wisely, and saying solemnly, "You know, Whitey, we're going to make a million."

When our lilies had been properly processed we took samples to an industrial laboratory at one of the universities to be analyzed, to find out if the stuff actually did possess that certain percentage of whatever George was looking for. For a couple of guys who were just on the brink of a million dollars we were very calm. We sat in the foyer of the school's chemical department discussing, with the dean of the college, our machinery and plant layout.

After we had exhausted this subject and the analysis was still not complete George and I sneaked next door to the Keg Room and had a couple of bracers. When we arrived back at the university the chemist told us that

the tests had been completed and before he gave us the results there would be a fee of two hundred pesos. What's two hundred pesos to a millionaire? He should have asked for three hundred. I dug into my wallet and came out with two one hundred pesos bills and handed them to the chemist. He made out a receipt which took three or four hundred years and then handed me the report of analysis. It said that George Parsons and Whitey Smith had one hundred by golly percent of pure unadulterated water lily ashes! George and I went back to the Keg Room for another bracer.

George got hold of my ear again and this time he almost bent it double. He said he didn't know what had gone wrong the first time but when it came to fertilizer he had the last word. We went to his house, and he got a can from his garage that was full of yellow adobe stone. George told me that there was no doubt that this stone contained that certain percentage of whatever he was looking for and that there was an unlimited supply of this stuff in the province of Albay.

I was convinced. I talked it over with my old friend Ray Higgins, and Ray cut himself in for fifteen hundred pesos.

George and I began to prospect. We found what George was sure contained that certain percentage and we were ready to mine. But we had no tools.

That evening there was a town fiesta and the mayor invited George and me as guests since we were the only two Americans in the town at that time. The mayor introduced us to the head engineer of the government's Department of Public Works and we all went in together to a little bar they had set up. The Public Works man got to be a real close friend.

The next day, George and I called on the engineer and he lent us picks, shovels, wheelbarrows and a steam roller and then moved half the city market to give us a place to roll down our yellow adobe stone. Ten days later, we had three hundred bags full, put them on a truck, took them to Manila and stored them in a borrowed warehouse. All except one bag, of course, which we took to the laboratory to have analyzed.

As soon as we had delivered the samples to the chemist George and I went next door to the Keg Room and when we had poured enough courage into ourselves we went back to the chemist to get the word. After I had paid the usual two hundred peso fee the chemist gave us the word and I felt like giving us back to him. Yes, sir, we had one hundred percent yellow adobe stone dust which we could have found on Dewey Boulevard, half a block away from the Manila Hotel!

When Whitey Smith makes up his mind to be a fertilizer tycoon, he's not going to stop at just two utter failures. I got hold of George Parsons again and we went back to Albay province. When we were there before, mining our yellow stone, adobe, one hundred per cent, an eighty-year-old bamboo American Spanish war veteran acted as kibitzer. He would stand around and cluck his tongue, tsk-tsking and making gloomy predictions.

"I don't hold much with your yellow adobe, but if it's fertilizer you want I know where you can get it."

He told us that farther up in the mountains there was a big three-chambered bat cave where thousands of generations of bats had been sleeping every day for thousands of years. He said there were hundreds of thousands of tons of bat guano there and all we had to do was dig it out.

George and I looked the old veteran up again and he arranged to take us to this fabulous bat cave where I was going to make my third million that month. We drove as far as we could and then hiked over the mountains. The eighty-year-old man kept getting ahead of us and was the first one to reach the caves. Then he gave us a briefing that I wished he had given us before we left and I would have gone back to Manila. He told us to be very careful because the cave was full of snakes – and don't talk too loud, he said, because there were hundreds of thousands of bats and if they got excited they would pick us to pieces.

He left us to mull this over and when I was just about to slither back over the mountains he returned with a dry banana tree to use as a torch. The old man carried the torch and the bucket and led the way in; George carried the shovel and I carried grave misgivings.

The deeper we went into the cave the deeper the guano became. It was like walking through a Louisiana swamp after a two and a half year rain. Every decade or so the old man would stop and shout back to us to be very quiet so we wouldn't wake the bats and then after that had echoed and reechoed several times, he hollered to be careful that we didn't step on the snakes.

I suggested that we go back, but the old man said no, there was one more chamber that contained another type of guano. Then the torch went out. I whispered to George, who had been digging samples all the time, "Haven't you got enough of this stuff yet?"

George hollered back, "Don't shout, Whitey, you'll wake up the bats." Then the old man had to add his two cents again and said in a stentorian voice, "Yeah, you'll wake the bats."

If the bats weren't awake by then they never would be. We made the long trek back without incident and so far as I know the bats are still slumbering on.

We rushed our samples back to the university. The chemist

knew me so well by this time that he collected the two hundred pesos before he made the analysis. But George and I were positive that we had that certain percentage he was looking for and when the chemist came out of his cubicle he was grinning. He told us the bat guano contained more than a certain percentage of whatever it was that George was looking for!

He told us it was really good fertilizer and would bring a good price. George and I looked at each other. It wasn't a gleam I saw in George's eye, it was a dollar sign. The chemist was still talking although he had quit grinning.

"But," he was saying, "you are a little late. The United Stated Government has just brought in two shiploads of commercial fertilizer as a gift from American taxpayers to the farmers of the Philippines If you fellows are figuring on going into business, forgot it. You can't compete with free fertilizer."

Very thoughtfully George went home. I went back to the Keg Room for a bracer.

Helen and I are happy and busy here in Manila. Somehow the friends we made in the darkest days of our lives, in Santo Tomas Internment Camp, seem closer and friendlier than anybody else we know. Old pals from the lush days of Shanghai, now scattered all over the world, are forever dropping in by ship or plane, reviving a million stories of old times and other people. We wine them and dine them – Helen, if i didn't mention it before, is a darn good cook.

Night life is as carefree and hectic as ever. We seem real close to Red China sometimes, and when a war scare comes along we wonder what will happen to us if it busts out again in Asia. I'm often reminded of the time when Clare Booth Luce sat in our Metro Bar and Grill watching the boys from the Army and the Navy whoop it up just before Pearl Harbor.

WHITEY SMITH

"Look at them," she said, "These men haven't the least worry about war and yet it is so close. Look at them dancing and drinking with not a care."

That's just about the way it is.

www.ingramcontent.com/pod-product-compliance
Ingram Content Group UK Ltd.
Pitfield, Milton Keynes, MK11 3LW, UK
UKHW040238250426
12048UKWH00043B/1572